FOLKLORE AND THE FANTASTIC IN TWELVE MODERN IRISH NOVELS

Recent Titles in Contributions to the
Study of Science Fiction and Fantasy

FOLKLORE AND THE FANTASTIC IN TWELVE MODERN IRISH NOVELS

cß

Marguerite Quintelli-Neary

Contributions to the Study of Science Fiction and Fantasy,
Number 76
C. W. Sullivan III, Series Adviser

Greenwood Press
Westport, Connecticut • London

PR
8807
.F27
Q56
1997

Library of Congress Cataloging-in-Publication Data

Quintelli-Neary, Marguerite, 1953–
    Folklore and the fantastic in twelve modern Irish novels /
Marguerite Quintelli-Neary.
        p.   cm.—(Contributions to the study of science fiction and
fantasy, ISSN 0193–6875 ; no. 76)
    Includes bibliographical references and index.
    ISBN 0–313–30490–4 (alk. paper)
    1. Fantastic fiction, English—Irish authors—History and
criticism.   2. Literature and folklore—Ireland—History—20th
century.   3. Joyce, James, 1882–1941—Knowledge—Folklore.
4. Mythology, Celtic, in literature.   5. Folklore in literature.
6. Heroes in literature.   I. Title.   II. Series.
PR8807.F27Q56   1997
823'.08766099415—dc21   97–13714

British Library Cataloguing in Publication Data is available.

Library of Congress Catalog Card Number: 97–13714
ISBN: 0–313–30490–4
ISSN: 0193–6875

First published in 1997

Greenwood Press, 88 Post Road West, Westport, CT 06881
An imprint of Greenwood Publishing Group, Inc.

Printed in the United States of America

The paper used in this book complies with the
Permanent Paper Standard issued by the National
Information Standards Organization (Z39.48–1984).

10 9 8 7 6 5 4 3 2 1

091098-27

Contents

CHAPTER 1

A Popular Culture: Irish Folklore and the Modern Irish Novel

The serious treatment accorded to heroic figures of Irish folklore in the works of late nineteenth-century and early twentieth-century Irish Renaissance writers such as William Butler Yeats and Lady Augusta Gregory could not be sustained very far into the twentieth century. Near religious fervor vis à vis traditional Gaelic writings would be supplanted by satirical and parodic handling of Irish mythological source works. The traditional Gaelic hero would alternately serve as political symbol and buffoon; and the chauvinism exhibited by chroniclers of a national mythology would be replaced by a purpose that more likely resembled that which inspired the tongue-in-cheek recorders of many medieval Irish tales—to amuse and entertain.

Modern folklorists contend that folklore encompasses many types of oral narratives, such as legends and folktales, as well as myths, but I will occasionally distinguish among these forms, prompted by definitions that Mary Helen Thuente established in *W. B. Yeats and Folklore*. She explains that folklore refers to a broad range of traditions that belonged to the nineteenth-century Irish peasantry, including narratives, songs, beliefs, and customs, while mythology includes narratives, songs, beliefs

and customs about ancient Irish gods and heroes, generally
found in written form in old manuscripts and in nineteenth-
century translations.[1]

The purpose behind my distinction among the sacred myth,
heroic legend, and secular regional folktale is not to assert the
authenticity or accuracy of one account versus another. My
intention is to demonstrate how modern Irish novelists, raised
in a tradition of orality combined with exposure to in-depth
scholarly research and findings, in both academic and popular
writing, used elements from myth and folklore to their own
purposes. Whether freely blending motifs from assorted source
works in fantasy writing or strictly imitating plot devices in
political or religious satire, they assert the uniquely Irish quality of their writing and evince their ability to recycle motifs
from well-worn tales.

Characters and themes from the novels in this study, which
date from 1912 to 1948, may be inspired by figures from ancient myths or medieval works, and they may appear in anachronistic combinations. As folklore began to subsume myth by
the nineteenth century, so literature of the twentieth century
subsumes both mythological and folklore traditions. Timeless
figures of the prehistoric tribes of the Mythological Cycle of
the goddess Danaan, of the Ulster Cycle of Conchobar and
Cuchulainn, situated at the time of Christ, and of the Fenian
legends of Fionn MacCumhaill, Oisin, and Oscar, which
dominated folklore by the sixteenth century, are refashioned to
suit the literary needs of the modern Irish novelist. John Mil-
lington Synge had already created a character, Christy Mahon,
in the tradition of the degenerate Oisin, in his 1907 drama, *The
Playboy of the Western World*, a work that appalled early audi-
ences by its representation of the peasantry but that also recalls
the traditional dispute between Oisin and St. Patrick. Recorded
by the twelfth century, the *Acallamh na Senorach*, or *Colloquy
of the Elders*, establishes the argument of a young hero who
wrestles with the voices of authority, and its renditions have

been modified to represent a mourning over the passing of pagan Ireland and the joyful acceptance of Christianity. But the continuation of motifs from Irish mythology and folklore is probably best accomplished in the genre of the novel, as seemingly complicitous writers James Stephens, James Joyce, and Flann O'Brien, as well as Mervyn Wall, Darrell Figgis, and Eimar O'Duffy, furnish us with their own adaptations of classical Irish hero tales.

If we interpret the treatment of mythological and folktale elements in the modern novel as an attempt to denigrate the tradition or rob it of its dignity, we are left with a limited understanding of the works; likewise, if we assert that each parallel development represents a conscious effort to preserve some aspect of Irish culture, we must assume the onerous task of proving the author's intent. My approach to the writers I have chosen to examine is to demonstrate how they have maintained two traditions of Irish literary culture: they carry on the traditions of parody and satire, as found in Swift, Carleton, Merriman, and the recorder of the *Vision of MacConglinne*, celebrate, in their role as modern mythmakers, many of the conventions found in tales of magic and heroism. It is valuable, too, to consider William R. Bascom's summary of the purposes of folklore in light of its effect on the modern Irish novel: it serves to validate culture, to educate, to maintain conformity, and to allow for escape in fantasy from repressions imposed on men by society.[2] Even parodic and self-conscious use of elements from folklore affirms its influence on the writer, for he either incorporates the motif directly in his literature as a recognizable artifact from popular culture (as Poe exploited phrenology and Mesmerism to generate horror fiction), or he exploits the folklore by altering its shape somewhat, leaving the reader with clues that range from the obvious to the near inscrutable. And, in order to function as innovative writers, modern novelists often incorporate a blend of elements from recorded myths and folktales in a single work, as was recently accomplished by

Desmond MacNamara in his 1994 *Book of Intrusions*, a late twentieth-century work of fiction that manages to add another parodic layer to Flann O'Brien's *At Swim-Two-Birds*, Brendan Behan's translation of *The Midnight Court*, and the medieval romance of Curither and Liadin, among other sources.[3] As Gerard Murphy points out, while *folklore* and *mythology* may not always be interchangeable terms, their themes are freely interchangeable.[4] Thus it is conceivable that, if themes from the epic *Tain bo Cuailgne* of the Ulster Cycle could reemerge in the Fenian Cycle, having undergone chronological adjustments, then thematic devices of early narrative tradition could be adapted to literature of the twentieth century. Joyce and other writers could transpose heroic characters of Irish folklore into contemporary heroes or antiheroes without concern for strict adherence to the original works. Use of the English language, as opposed to the Gaelic language, might even prompt word invention for concepts that are alien to the English tongue, whether for serious purposes or in the comic mode. Certainly, Flann O'Brien, who wrote in both tongues, had a gift for word invention, and Joyce's famed fascination with wordplay has inspired readers to comment that he is not actually writing, at all times, in English. Along with inventive use of language, the modern writers avail themselves of contemporary settings, which obviate a literal interpretation of elements from folklore or euhemeristic approaches to myth.

The novelists I have chosen all exhibit a fascination and a familiarity with Celtic elements or at least with the popularity of Celtic motifs. As Charles W. Sullivan III explains, after Synge, Eliot, and Joyce, intoxication with features of Irish traditional writing may be found in the works of fantasy writers who are creators of impossible, Secondary Worlds, in which there is a presumed "happy ending" or "a noble struggle in defeat."[5] While fantasy applies to the works of Wall, Figgis, O'Brien, and O'Duffy, the most fantastic episodes of Joyce's *Ulysses* (1922) and the dream setting of *Finnegans Wake* (1939) are stylistically closer to Celtic source works and removed in tone and spirit from Stephens' world of leprechauns. As Maria Tymoczko observes in her thorough study of *Ulysses* and Irish tradition, Joyce mimics the parodic listing and lore in the tradition of *Vision of MacConglinne* and maintains the alliterative device of medieval transcripts.[6]

There are countless strategies for replenishing myth and folklore, just as there may be unlimited variations on a literary theme. There were, likewise, many recorders of tales within the Gaelic tradition of storytelling and a variety of methods of narration. The *ollamh*, or bardic tradition, had nine divisions, including historians, keepers of genealogies, poets or *fili*, writers of heroic stories or *loidhe*, judges of the people, teachers of wit, wisdom, and satire, and tellers of tales. The *seanachie* was entrusted with the historical tales, of which he had to know 178.[7] The modern novelist could serve as any one or a combination of several of these storytellers, alternately recording his literary, fictional tale, reciting genealogy in parodic fashion, and constructing a wandering hero tale, as Joyce does in *Ulysses*. Or he may introduce a traditional *seanachie* into his own plot structure, as Figgis does in *The Return of the Hero* (1923), reserving the role of outer storyteller for himself.

But if we cannot immediately recognize the classification of storyteller the author adopts, we may observe other connections between the abilities, flaws, values, and conflicts of the literary heroes and those of Irish tradition. In order to establish links between the warrior hero Cuchulainn of the Ulster Cycle, whose exploits were not recorded until the eighth century, and the twentieth-century working man, Leopold Bloom of *Ulysses*, we have to examine thematic and structural similarities between the characters created by the earliest chroniclers of Irish myth, eighteenth- and nineteenth-century transcribers and translators, and twentieth-century novelists. And, because there is often a multiplicity of themes in a given work, the onus of determining which are its salient features falls upon the

translator/scribe. The modern-age writer assimilates that which
has been stressed in both scholarly and popular writings, so
that he may inadvertently perpetuate a motif that may have
been irrelevant or nonexistent. But because, like metahistory,
most of the events recounted in myths and hero tales either
occurred quite differently or never really happened at all, the
repetition of their motifs in a literary frame emphasizes the
need for a national mythology and, with it, a distinctive identity.

Because the six writers I have chosen, with the exception of
Figgis, do not come close to a literal retelling of any traditional
Irish tale, I do not apply a complete set of folktale precepts to
each work. The random though abundant use of allusions to
early Irish works, the elasticity of time and space, and the characteristics they assign to their heroes signal the writers' interest
in creating uniquely Irish fiction.

STRUCTURE

Although Vladimir Propp's 1958 study *A Morphology of the
Folktale* applies to Russian fairy tales, their plots, and character
types, he makes a useful distinction between structure and
theme which may be beneficial when discussing Irish folklore.
Propp explains that all that is predicate denotes structure (i.e.,
what the hero does or what is done to him); all other parts of
the sentence provide us with theme (who the hero is, upon
whom he acts or who acts upon him, what he is like).[8] Thus
Flann O'Brien's *At Swim-Two-Birds* structurally resembles Fenian legend in that the writer hero, like the poet Fionn, actively seeks truth or knowledge. The structure of Mervyn
Wall's Fursey tale is Fenian, too, because the hero's bride is
stolen from him, as was MacCumhaill's bride in the Diarmaid
and Grainne legend.

The Celtic hero nearly always actively participates in all of
his life's events, including his own birth, an occurrence that
would normally be considered a passive one. The recounting

of the heroic birth can be so dramatic, given the miraculous circumstances that surround it, that the hero appears to have effected it himself. Some of the prenatal events may be hazy, unknown, or hinting at divine origin, and there is rarely a normal period of gestation. In the Ulster Cycle, Conchobar, son of Nes and Cathbad, the sorcerer, is carried for three years and three months; Cuchulainn is born as the "son of three years" to Conchobar's sister Dechtire, after another allegedly incestuously conceived fetus is aborted; Fionn MacCumhaill's parents are often described as having disappeared after he was born, or his mother, Muirne of the White Neck, must steal away with the infant after the murder of his father, Cumhaill. While the hero of Celtic narrative tradition may not be born to ordinary, mortal parents, and his birth circumstances may assume features of Christian mythology, it is interesting to examine how the modern Irish novelist translates this concept.

Flann O'Brien often removes the hero's parents very early from the scene, as though most children were orphaned at a young age. The narrator of *The Third Policeman* (1940) briefly alludes to his parents' untimely demise; the university student of *At Swim-Two-Birds* (1939) resides with an uncle. O'Brien also creates, in the latter work, a hero who is born fully grown through what he names "aestho-psycho-eugenics," a process that may measure up to the divine origins of mythology, as well as chillingly recall Hitlerian genetic dynamics. Eimar O'Duffy provides for heroic births in edenic settings in *King Goshawk and the Birds* (1926) when the visiting hero's offspring, Cuandine, emerges from the womb with five years' knowledge in Tir na nOg, or Land of the Young.

This earliest structural phase of heroic life, beyond the character's control to some degree, serves to prepare for the next active stage of the hero's life, that of leaving the familiar world of parents and being nurtured or adopted by fosterers. The helper figures actually enable the hero to assume a life of isolation and independence. Cuchulainn is raised by other clan

members and taught to despise customs and royal authority;
Fionn MacCumhaill joins the *fian*, a tribe of hunters or mer-
cenaries who live apart from society. The hero is further re-
named upon an appropriate occasion, as Cuchulainn, origi-
nally named Setanta, acquires his new kenning-like title after
slaying the hound of Culann; Fionn MacCumhaill, once called
Demne, acquires his heroic name after he tastes of the cooking
salmon.

While the practice of sending children off to boarding
school was certainly not unusual to upper middle-class Anglo-
Irish citizens of the late nineteenth century, Joyce's treatment
of the separation from family in *A Portrait of the Artist as a
Young Man* (1914) emphasizes the intrusion of extrafamilial
figures in the life of Stephen Dedalus, who would enter *Ulysses*
(1922) as the rebellious non conformist who has removed himself physically from his family and separated himself philo-
sophically from his Jesuit instructors. The Philosophers in
Stephens' *Crock of Gold* (1914) exchange their children;
O'Duffy sends Cuandine of *King Goshawk and the Birds* (1926)
to the different heavens for his first ten years to be instructed
in the code of the Gaelic hero.

Dissociation from the enclave of the family identifies the
hero and fosters a third structural convention, that of the
macgnimartha, or education of the hero. The education may be
pagan, monastic, in a Catholic setting, or scholastic, in a secular
setting, but it extends beyond that which is received by ordinary children; and it is during this process that the hero learns
of what separates him from others. In traditional writings, the
hero becomes aware of his peculiarity, a physical or mental
ability, though it may also be a handicap, at this stage of his
education.

Cuchulainn may assume incredible strength and manifest
physical distortions; Fionn MacCumhaill, also gigantic in stature, receives knowledge whenever he puts his thumb in his
mouth. In a modern novel, O'Brien's DeSelby, first introduced

in *The Third Policeman* (1940), has the gift of extraordinary knowledge and later travels beneath the sea to hold conversations with deceased saints in *The Dalkey Archive* (1964). In Mervyn Wall's *The Return of Fursey* (1948), Fursey is given limited powers of wizardry as well as the gift of a canine familiar.

But the discovery of the possession of a peculiarity in an Irish hero is generally offset by the pronouncement of an interdiction or prohibition of some sort. Marie-Louise Sjoestedt-Jonval stresses that this Celtic *geis* differs from taboo in that it is the character who must not interact with a certain object or person that is accentuated, rather than the object or person to be avoided.[9] Thus, while it is dangerous for Cuchulainn to eat the flesh of a dog, it is not necessarily a problem for anyone else. Celtic lore often speaks of the mother pronouncing this *geis*, and Joyce therefore appears to repeat the structural device with Stephen Dedalus' mother's dying request (though, inversely, she wants him not to avoid agents but to commit action, by praying for her), but a prohibition may also be pronounced by a sage or druid. Some heroes are given injunctions that only they may fulfill, commands that exert the pressures of upholding *geis*. Cuchulainn is expected to slaughter certain birds that fly overhead and to catch certain fish, for example. In a modern literary work, O'Duffy's Cuandine is sent back to earth to free the songbirds.

Violations of *geasa*, or failure to carry out injunctions, traditionally lead to a hero's downfall, though young Fionn's taboo breaking via touching of the cooking salmon leads to the acquisition of *imbas forosna*, or illuminating knowledge. This reversal of fortune may occur because he intends to keep it from burning, or, possibly, as suggested by Elliott B. Gose Jr., because he asserts himself in this wonder tale (a similar behavior in the context of mythology would have precipitated certain doom).[10] Joyce's literary hero suffers the psychological consequences of refusing a mother's request/pronouncement, assuming the burden of guilt he names *agenbite of inwit*, from

the medieval tradition. Conversely, when James Stephens'
tinker, in *The Demi-Gods* (1914), provides for proper burial of
the dead, he fulfills an injunction common to many Irish folktales and gains peace of mind through his gesture of respect.
Whether related to pagan taboos or Christian sins, interdictions and injunctions in Irish folklore and literature always
affect heroic status.

One special type of interdiction that occurs in Celtic and
other folklores, though not always expressly pronounced, is
that against the hero's involvement with females. Association
with the female sex almost always leads to negative repercussions, undermining the hero's standing or causing suffering to
others. Medb eggs on her husband Aillil in the epic *Tain*, pro-
moting the war in which Cuchulainn emerges the hero; out of
jealousy over Grainne, Fionn MacCumhaill has his friend
Diarmaid killed in a boar hunt; and it is through the seduction
of Niamh of the Golden Hair that Oisin abandons his father,
Fionn, in his hour of need and steals off to Tir na nOg. Joseph
Nagy indicates that women disrupt the order of Fionn's tribe
and pit the bandits against each other in Fenian Cycle tales.[11]
Females link heroes with the social world in the Ulidian Cycle
in that an arrangement must be made immediately after Cuchulainn's wedding to Emer, so that she must not, as dictated by
law, offer her virginity first to the king, thereby enraging
Cuchulainn and leading to murder and destruction. Even if
interaction with females creates limited disorder, it does not
appear to enhance the hero's status; indeed, women generally
cause Celtic heroes to operate as members of a flawed society.
And, while it is possible that monastic recordings of so many
oral tales may be blamed for the negative image of women, one
that derives from biblical sources, the structural pattern of
women's impact on heroic actions prevails in the modern Irish
novel.

The irresistible female, Sheila Lamont, bewitches Dermot
Trellis of O'Brien's *At Swim-Two-Birds*, so that the character is

unable to control himself and rapes her. Later he is put on trial and humiliated by his son, a pattern of sexual misconduct/trial/mortification that is reverberated in Joyce's *Finnegans Wake*. The alluring Molly Bloom of *Ulysses* causes her husband to spend much of his day masochistically torturing himself with thoughts of her presumed affairs, although, as Tymoczko rightly observes, there is a tolerance of this adultery, which gives Molly kinship with Medb because "the impetus to union—particularly in a sovereign figure—is natural."[12] The once-lovely Maeve of Wall's *Return of Fursey* causes the hero countless indignities and hardships as he tries to recapture her. Like his mythological counterpart, when the Irish literary hero succumbs to feminine enticements, he pays a price: he abandons nobler objectives and suffers physical and/or mental pain. Cumhaill of Fenian lore dies when he marries, as prophesied; Leopold Bloom of *Ulysses*, a modern hero, is domesticated and forced to conform, albeit willingly, to society's norms.

Not only must the Irish hero resist feminine wiles, but he must also undergo tests and trials, assuredly a universal motif in hero sagas. These include visitations to the Otherworld, the *sidhe*, or fairy mounds, imprisonment or confinement, and confrontation with trickster figures, some of which occur simultaneously. Cuchulainn must voyage to the feasting hall, or *bruidne*, of Forgall, ostensibly to meet the challenge of his future father-in-law and to woo Emer, but concurrently completing one of his required trips to the Otherworld.[13] His undoing is brought about by sorcery, when he is tricked into eating dog flesh, as prophesied. Fionn MacCumhaill is frequently shown crossing the threshold to the land of the fairies or drinking from the well of the Otherworld as a means of acquiring illuminating knowledge. In the *bruidhean* tales of Fionn, the hero often finds himself trapped in magical dwellings or pitted against druids and magicians, and it is in these situations that he is most vincible.[14] His son Oisin is allegedly tricked into deserting his father, as mentioned above, and following Niamh to

Tir na nOg, to return to christianized Ireland three hundred years later, a withered and wandering blind man.

Visits to the Otherworld and social and sexual intercourse among humans and non humans may seem less plausible in modern novels, unless they are works of science fiction, yet several modern Irish novelists have preserved the formalistic devices of narrative tradition in their works. Their heroes are entrapped, betrayed, and put on trial in nightmarish Otherworlds. Yet the Irish novels differ from other modern works with similar goings-on that take place in dream sequences, in that their Otherworlds are frequently peopled with figures from Gaelic mythological and folklore sources, or in that their heroes have been banished to these other worlds because they failed to maintain *geis* or carry out injunctions. Stephen Dedalus, locked out of Martello Tower from the first division of *Ulysses*, already bears the remorse of a *genbite of inwit*. He is exposed, along with Bloom, to unearthly visions in the "Circe" episode, in which the latter receives punishment for breaking sexual *geasa*. H. C. Earwicker, in Joyce's *Finnegans Wake*, is put on trial with a jury composed of his own pub customers, and he remains a prisoner in his own dreamworld, in which his subconscious mind and the dream censor struggle to gain a stronghold in his mythic creation. Wall's Fursey is banished from his monastery for trafficking with Satan, harassed by the devil himself, and tortured by wizards. O'Brien's Dermot Trellis (*At Swim-Two-Birds*), victimized by his own characters, who seize control of the plot when he falls asleep, recalls the poet of the satirical *Midnight Court*, in which authorial control slips away. Trellis visits a *sidhe* of his own making, peopled with a pooka, cinema stars, Finn MacCool, and ordinary humans.

But Celtic heroes of folklore and literature need not always go "beyond the door" to engage in battle. Some conflicts are resolved through a show of physical strength, as in Cuchulainn's battle with the god Bolga (Oengus Bolg) or in his singlehanded defeat of the provinces of Connacht, Leinster, Munster, and Ulster in the *Tain*. Fionn MacCumhaill must seek retribution against Goll MacMorna (Aedh) for the killing of his father, Cumhaill. Sjoestedt-Jonval reminds us that one of the terms for Celtic hero, *laech*, means "he who carries arms."[15] Thus Cuchulainn first distinguishes himself as a warrior, then as a wise man; and Fionn MacCumhaill spends more time in hunt and battle than in seeking knowledge. The physical threats surrounding the hero of antiquity, however, outnumber those that the modern literary hero faces.

We cannot expect the hero of the modern Irish novel to slay real monsters, hunt boars, or ward off foreign invaders (although Wall's Fursey makes great efforts to protect the monastery of Clonmacnoise from a Viking attack, and O'Duffy's Cuandine leads valiantly in battle), but he must engage in struggle all the same. Some of the literary battles occur in the face of discrimination or financial hardship. Joyce offers anti-Semitism in *Ulysses* as a challenge to Dedalus and a burden to Bloom; Figgis has Oisin confront narrowmindedness as he defends his father's pure intentions in *The Return of the Hero*.

While some conflicts appear alien to the struggles of traditional Irish hero figures, there are, in the modern Irish novel, other ongoing or unresolved dilemmas that span the centuries and ally the old tales with the new. There exists, in Irish storytelling, an ever-present discord between father and son, which may also stand as a metaphor for paganism versus Christianity, hedonism versus asceticism, stagnation versus progress, or, as David Krause suggests, the artistic imagination versus religious fervor.[16] Perhaps no other structural device binds the traditional Irish narrative with the modern Irish novel as strongly as that of the irresolvable argument between the forces of preservation (the father) and those of destruction (the son). In the Ulster Cycle, the establishment of the new order through takeover by the son is averted when Cuchulainn unknowingly slays Conglaech, the product of his union with Aife. In the

Fenian Cycle, Oisin displays a rebellious *non-serviam* attitude
when he does verbal battle with St. Patrick, a surrogate father,
in the *Acallamh na Senorach*,[17] and there are numerous versions
of the argument's outcome, although Christianity finally
emerges victorious over paganism. It is not as essential that one
side or the other win the argument as it is that the shift in balance perpetuate itself.

In a modern literary context, Dermot Trellis (of O'Brien's
At Swim-Two-Birds), who thinks he is in control of his own
novel, may be browbeaten by characters of his own creation.
In the same work, Orlick Trellis, Dermot's adult-born son, via
the process of aestho-psycho-eugenics, represents a modern-day
equivalent of the three-hundred-year-old child-man Oisin with
whom St. Patrick patiently engages in repartee. When
O'Duffy's displaced character, O'Kennedy, of *The Spacious
Adventures of the Man in the Street* (1928), attempts to explain
Earth ways to the Ratheans, it soon dawns on him that the old
rules no longer apply. These literary devices, while physically
impossible in the real world, serve to disequilibrate an established order, whether it is authorial control, religious dogma,
or unfamiliar mores.

While Stephen Dedalus had apparently resolved the di-
lemma of religious vocation versus artistic expression in *Portrait of the Artist*, electing to become a "priest" of artistic creation, he continues to resist suppression of the clergy, in *Ulysses*,
and clings tenaciously to the forms of ritual, as he questions
the possibility of being one's own father.

If the deepest conflicts of traditional Irish narratives appear
to possess a dual nature, then they mirror thematic similarities
among the works. Celtic heroes both win by losing and maintain their ground by giving way, for there is a division in their
nature. It is difficult to provide a strict separation of structure
and theme in that the hero's personality generally prompts
him to behave in a certain way (although how he is acted upon
may be beyond his control or dictated by prophesy). But there

are many descriptive qualities that characterize the hero and may be examined in isolation and later connected to the chain of heroic actions. These qualities demonstrate how closely the hero of the modern Irish novel resembles his folklore prototype, in both character traits and physical attributes.

THEME

While structural considerations deal with actions performed by or upon the hero, thematic ones treat the nature of the hero and his cohorts. The hero is variously identified by his goals or mandates, his family or clan, as well as by his fosterers, and by his sets of values. The last of these, possessing a dual nature, imparts a quasi-schizophrenic quality to the hero, who pragmatically hunts and protects the tribe (as do Cuchulainn and Fionn, shielding their men from foreign invasions instigated by Vikings and dwellers of the *sidhe*) and undergoes a poet's training. Fionn MacCumhaill, whom Sjoestedt-Jonval calls "the living negation of tribal institutions,"[18] reveals the *fili*/poet side of his nature as he quests for the truth. Unlike Cuchulainn, who was already blessed with the gifts of counsel and beautiful speech, among his fifteen peculiarities, Fionn must be instructed in these qualities, and he remains on the boundary of society. It is Joseph Nagy's thesis that the characteristics of *fili* (poet) and *fennid* (warrior) merge in the heroic Fionn MacCumhaill, and it is also this duality that provides a prototype for the modern Irish literary hero.[19]

A character who is a poet or seeker of truth, with the gift of foresight or superhuman intuition, does not fit into mainstream society. Conflicts naturally result when the *fili*/poet must operate and survive in the modern world, and Joyce resolves the conflict to some degree by creating a composite Celtic hero in *Ulysses*. He accomplishes this via the fusion of Stephen Dedalus and Leopold Bloom, both of whom live with vacillating proportions of *fili*/poet and *fennid*/worker qualities, and though lasting union is never actually affirmed, Joyce suggests the possibility of a balance in their encounters. Further, the composite hero symbolizes the multilayered father-son conflict of Irish tradition. We have, on the one hand, a character (in Bloom) who is linked with all and sensitive to some of the other characters he meets during the course of his odyssey in *Ulysses*, one who functions as a socially adjusted individual. He, in turn, interacts with a younger, socially alienated individual (Stephen Dedalus), who has rejected his biological father and set off to become a seeker of wisdom. While they appear to represent opposite sides of a dual-natured character, they are both wanderers in pursuit of knowledge who operate mentally on the fringe of society. Ironically, Dedalus, who pursues nonconformity, is more readily embraced by Irish society, while Bloom, who seeks to conform, is rebuffed.

Boundaries of ethnic heritage and religion separate Bloom from complete social union, while philosophical and political differences alienate Dedalus. Like Oisin, Dedalus is wary of allying himself with social organizations; Oisin relentlessly maintains his pro-pagan position in the "Dialogues" with St. Patrick and joins the Fenian heroes in hell after the failed attempt to rescue. Perhaps the same motivation, the need to preserve poet/outcast qualities, prompts Dedalus to refuse to sign the testimonial to the czar of Russia in *Portrait of the Artist*.

When Fionn MacCumhaill allows jealousy to overtake him and permits the killing of his beloved friend Diarmaid, he has bought into conformist values and sacrificed his rebel position. Similarly, the literary Bloom succumbs to human frailties when he lingers on reflections about his wife's love life, reminding us that he is bound to the social conventions of marriage. The Celtic hero is continually drawn into a world of conformity, trying to keep one foot in each world without completely sacrificing his independence. But the hero of myth and folklore may receive protection from internal and external forces that threaten his special status, for he has been granted extrahuman qualities during his heroic education.

Otherwordly peculiarities may manifest themselves in the form of superhuman physical prowess, mental acuity, metamorphosis, or, inversely (in the literary mode), by physical deformity. These qualities may serve to preserve or enhance the *fili* or *fennid* side of the hero's nature or shield him from the forces of conformity.

In the Mythological Cycle, Lugh ("The Bright One," a possible divine source for Fionn MacCumhaill) is said to destroy his enemies by staring at them and to be able to jump on a bubble without bursting it (the former of these gifts apparently being more useful). Like Fionn, he fights a one-eyed opponent, Balor, of the Otherworld. Cuchulainn possesses seven fingers on each hand, seven toes on each foot, a hero-halo, tricolored hair, and the ability to contort his body in terrifying and grotesque ways. Already blessed with knowledge, his skills at warfare are increased through these devices. James MacKillop notes that Fionn MacCumhaill acts as a peripheral figure in action, benefiting from benevolent helpers such as the *ceadach*.[20] But on a mental level, he has but to put his finger in his mouth, or drink from the magical water of a certain well, or from Ciulenn's cup, and he receives *imbas forosnai*. In order to fight off the forces of adversity, the Celtic hero relies on features that distinguish him from ordinary mortals.

Fantastic abilities also appear in works of modern Irish literature. Flann O'Brien introduces extrahuman characteristics freely in his novels: DeSelby (*The Third Policeman* and *The Dalkey Archive*) claims to have conquered time; fictional characters are brought to life through "aestho-autogamy" (*At Swim-Two-Birds*); and a narrator converses telepathically with the dead (*The Third Policeman*). Mervyn Wall allows Fursey to summon up a familiar in the form of a dog, who provides him with refreshment when he is called (*The Return of Fursey*), just as Fionn's obedient dog Bran stays by his side, although Wall creates a variation on the theme when the familiar begins to dominate the hero.

Where some Irish literary heroes are singled out by extraordinary endowments, Joyce chooses to introduce deformity or
deprivation. Stephen Dedalus symbolically "handicaps" himself, tapping his way to the tower early on in *Ulysses*. This motif combines the tradition of the blind poet/prophet
(Homer/Tiresias) who sees, with the Irish association of the
wood with the life force and the Ossianic motif of the blind
wanderer. O'Brien also makes use of deformity, providing the
narrator of *The Third Policeman* with a wooden leg. While
such disabilities do not assist the hero in times of trial, they do
indicate that he is of special rank.

One of the most interesting peculiarities that has been trans-
literated from Irish folklore to the modern novel is the ability
to metamorphose. This thematic element occurs freely in the
"Circe" episode of *Ulysses*, where male and female figures inter-
change roles and we are reminded of the medieval Fenian tale,
"The Feast of Conan's House," in which a warrior is a woman
one year and a man the next, bearing children as a woman and
siring them as a man.[21] O'Brien also alludes to gender confusion or role exchange when Miss Lamont is discussed as both a
woman and a man in *At Swim-Two-Birds*, but he offers an even
more unusual situation of metamorphosis in *The Third Policeman* and *The Dalkey Archive*. In these novels it is proposed that
a bicycle can become part human, and a man, part bicycle,
through the "exchange of molecules" theory. O'Duffy has
Cuchulainn assume the shopworker O'Kennedy's body, so
that the partially deceased mortal must find a new shell to live
in, providing for a blend of metempsychosis and metamorphosis.

Superhuman powers or unusual marks also serve to identify
the hero, as does the burdensome device of *geis*. Because he
must heed the warnings, the hero is consumed by an unusual
fear, often associated with a common object that would not
ordinarily pose a threat to anyone. Cuchulainn must look out
for the dog that will be his undoing; Fionn must be on the

alert for trickster figures. Women are generally to be feared in Fenian tales, for they are either half-human and half-animal or half-supernatural.[22] But, because the Celtic hero is braver than he is fearful, he often ignores his own sense of foreboding or is deceived into not recognizing the object he should fear. Sjoestedt-Jonval refers to the intense bravery of the Celts as "suicidal excess,"[23] and this valor is part of what makes the hero vulnerable. Fionn ultimately receives five wounds in death, a decidedly Christian symbolism (although his dying is not generally mentioned in the oral tradition), and Cuchulainn is filled with holes before he dies. When trepidation is overcome by reckless bravery, the hero's vulnerability increases.

The frailties of fear and openness to attack often translate as phobias or obsessions in the modern Irish novel. Stephen Dedalus unnaturally fears water in *Ulysses*, an imbalance that is offset by Bloom's extreme love of the element. While hydrophobia may reflect the author's childhood experience of near drowning, it more likely symbolizes fear of baptismal water (representing communion with society) or the feminine. When Stephen remarks that all of Ireland is washed by the sea, he may express fear of capitulation through baptism.

While water often represents fertility and rebirth in folklore, it is also associated with incidents of near drowning. And, in ancient Irish mythology, water may be connected to intuitive knowledge and, as such, would be female in nature.[24] Where Fionn MacCumhaill learns that he may acquire knowledge when he drinks the water of the Otherworld, Stephen Dedalus of *Ulysses* may fear that total immersion will force unwanted knowledge upon him, the knowledge brought by societal integration. His fear, therefore, makes him braver in his resistance to communion, but it also increases his vulnerablity as he remains isolated.

The price that the hero of Irish traditional writings and the modern Irish novel must pay for individuality may be relative isolation, but the reward is the ability to exist in two intellec-

tual and physical worlds. This complex nature supports
Claude Lévi-Strauss' thesis that primitive peoples were capable
of disinterested thinking when they created myths of a highly
intellectual nature.[25] When the earliest mythmakers and storytellers fashioned their narratives, providing for a hero who is
courageous but fearful, strong but vulnerable, and mortal but
extrahuman (or divine but bearing human traits), they were
providing the blueprint for structural and thematic motifs that
could be imitated in modern literature. The presence of so
many of these motifs in the works of Stephens, Joyce, and succeeding writers, while occasionally coincidental, is too powerful to be ignored.

STRATEGIES

Where obvious allusions to the structure and themes of Irish
source tales occur, they are generally satirical or parodic in nature. The writers blatantly replenish devices of myth and folklore as they rework them in contemporary narratives. Joyce
includes a variety of metamorphic possibilities for HCE in
Finnegans Wake, incorporating a salmon in the River Liffey
(from Ulidian lore, or the Ulster Cycle) and Finn MacCool
(from Fenian lore). In the "Cyclops" episode of *Ulysses*, he
parodies nineteenth-century translations of Gaelic literature
derived from folklore, through a dog, Garryowen, who can
supposedly recite verse in Gaelic. O'Brien also inserts obvious
references to Celtic folklore in *At Swim-Two-Birds*, by introducing Finn MacCool and a real pooka and through the strong
resemblance between characters' names and their folklore
sources: Dermot, a derivative of Diarmaid, and Sheila Lamont,
a voluptuous female whose name may be linked to the Irish
fertility goddess, Sheela-na-gig. Further, when O'Brien introduces his narratives in the first person, he preserves a method
of narration used for all Irish ballads of the seventeenth
through nineteenth centuries, one that distinguishes them from
ballads of continental Europe and England.[26] While this per-

sonalized rhetoric may appear to involve the reader more fully in the text, it is nonetheless a traditional Irish narrative device. When Joyce interrupts narration in *Ulysses*, via authorial intrusion, the strategy is frequently viewed as yet another of the experimental styles employed in the work. Yet it, too, is a device used by the native Irish *seanachie*, who interrupts his tale to insert a personal opinion or to aver that what he recounts is true. As all Irish tales were meant to be narrated aloud or chanted, and all ballads sung or recited, it is logical that the teller of the tale would pause to embroider his narration.

In addition to devices of narration, there are other, less familiar elements in twentieth-century Irish novels that recall features of folklore. O'Brien's mad Sweeny of *At Swim-Two-Birds*, explained within the text as a saint gone mad, changed into a bird, and said to have flown up into a tree, actually derives from an Irish legend of Merlin. A character known as Suibhne to the Irish, he went insane after the Battle of Moira, thinking himself responsible for the slain soldiers, flew to the top of a tree, and, after being begged to come down, disappeared into the clouds. And, as Thomas O'Grady convincingly demonstrates in *"At Swim-Two-Birds* and the Bardic Schools,"* O'Brien's learned narrator keeps to his bedchamber in the tradition of the secluded bard, who is exhorted to compose his poetry in darkness and to eschew the outdoors, another device that links the novel to medieval Irish tradition.[27] And Wall very likely utilizes legends that surround a St. Fursa, or Fursey, a seventh-century monk who founded a monastery in France, as a source for his monastic hero.

The operation of motifs from traditional Irish folklore on apparent and more intricate levels in the modern Irish novel can be explored to the point of exhaustion. The writers may employ allusions and imitative patterns of structure and theme for a variety of purposes, and the precision with which they implement these devices often depends on whether their knowledge derives from childhood recollections, contemporary readings of investigative research on folklore, or scholarly pursuits. But the repetition of devices, even in moments of high comedy and farce, reaffirms the importance of narrative traditions in Irish literary history.

NOTES

1. Mary Helen Thuente, *W. B. Yeats and Folklore* (Totowa, N.J.: Barnes and Noble, 1980), pp. 2-3.

2. Alan Dundes, *The Study of Folklore* (Englewood Cliffs, N.J.: Prentice-Hall, Inc., 1965), pp. 290-294.

3. Marguerite Quintelli-Neary, "Desmond MacNamara's Intrusions and Invasions," *Notes on Modern Irish Literature* 8 (1996), p. 29.

4. Gerard Murphy, *The Ossianic Lore and Romantic Tales of Medieval Ireland* (Dublin: Colm O. Lochlainn, 1961), p. 52.

5. Charles W. Sullivan III, *Welsh Celtic Myth in Modern Fantasy* (Westport, Conn.: Greenwood Press, 1989), p. 144.

6. Maria Tymoczko, *The Irish Ulysses* (Berkeley: University of California Press, 1994), p. 151.

7. Ruth Sawyer, *The Way of the Storyteller* (Middlesex, Eng.: Penguin, 1942), p. 65.

8. Vladimir Propp, *Morphology of the Folktale*, 2nd ed. (1958; rpt. Austin: University of Texas Press, 1968), p. 113.

9. Marie-Louise Sjoestedt-Jonval, *Dieux et héros des celtes* (Paris: Presses universitaires de France, 1940), p. 96.

10. Elliott B. Gose Jr., *The World of the Irish Wonder Tale* (Toronto: University of Toronto Press, 1985), p. 85.

11. Joseph Falaky Nagy, *The Wisdom of the Outlaw* (Berkeley: University of California Press, 1985), p. 73.

12. Tymoczko, *The Irish Ulysses*, p. 123.

13. Thomas O'Rahilly, *Early Irish History and Mythology* (1946; rpt. Dublin: Dublin Institute for Advanced Studies, 1971), p. 124.

14. James MacKillop, *Fionn MacCumhaill: Celtic Myth in English Literature* (Syracuse: Syracuse University Press, 1986), p. 24.

15. Sjoestedt-Jonval, *Dieux et héros des celtes*, p. 80.

16. David Krause, *The Profane Book of Irish Comedy* (Ithaca, N.Y.: Cornell University Press, 1982), p. 80.

17. Ibid, p. 62.

18. Sjoestedt-Jonval, *Dieux et héros des celtes*, p. 110.

19. Nagy, *The Wisdom of the Outlaw*, p. 18.

20. MacKillop, *Fionn MacCumhaill*, p. 25.

21. Nagy, *The Wisdom of the Outlaw*, p. 51.

22. Ibid., p. 95.

23. Sjoestedt-Jonval, *Dieux et héros des celtes*, p. 94.

24. Nagy, *The Wisdom of the Outlaw*, p. 111.

25. Claude Lévi-Strauss, *Myth and Meaning* (New York: Shocken, 1979), p. 18.

26. Murphy, *Ossianic Lore and Romantic Tales*, p. 21.

27. Thomas B. O'Grady, "*At Swim-Two-Birds* and the Bardic Schools," *Éire/Ireland* 24, 3 (Fall 1989), p. 71.

CHAPTER 2

Ulysses and Celtic Parallels

Ever since Stuart Gilbert's schematic study of James Joyce's *Ulysses* appeared in 1930, explicating the novel as a modern Irish parallel of Homer's *Odyssey*, criticism has focused on its similarities to the Greek epic. The eighteen divisions of *Ulysses* correspond, more or less, to eighteen of the twenty-four divisions in the Homeric epic. Yet the deletion of the headings in the final manuscript of *Ulysses* indicates that Joyce's novel had undergone many stylistic and thematic changes during the eight years he worked on it. As Zack Bowen points out, the Gilbert schema may provide problems in interpreting the final version of *Ulysses* because of the ongoing changes in technique during its composition.[1]

The Odyssean headings are therefore best used as a measure of convenience when delineating chapters only because they have dominated critical discussion of the work for so many years.

Fortunately, recent critical work has changed emphasis in an approach to *Ulysses*, notably with the work of Maria Tymoczko, whose exhaustive study of its "Irishness," in *The Irish Ulysses*, imparts unity to it as an Irish novel. Earlier scholarly essays and studies had briefly referred to Hibernian motifs and allusions in the novel; but a rethinking of its structure and themes allows us to make a case for interpreting the novel as a reworking of Irish myth in an urban setting. The universal qualities of the Hellenic source work need not obscure the parallels to Irish legends. While there are assuredly plot devices and thematic concerns that emerge in the epic works of many cultures, there are peculiarly Irish or, more important, stereotypically Irish ones that are found in *Ulysses*.

Not only do Irish mythic parallels abound in *Ulysses*, but they are strengthened by the intrusion of Christian myth, which impacted Ireland politically and socially. Irish folklore absorbs Christian elements without apparent conflict of interest; the goddess Brigid gives way to St. Bridget as legends are "updated." Similarly, Joyce parodies the Celtic Revival, with its feverish attempts to recapture a golden past, along with Catholic doctrine, which seeks to negate Irish pagan heritage. Anthony Burgess' assertion that Joyce's Irishry was "passive," "innate," and "unpromoted"[2] fails to entertain a certain irony: the harder Joyce tried to sublimate or mock Gaelic hero tales and their role in Irish culture, the more he validated them through repetition of theme and structure.

It is known that Joyce had studied de Jubainville's work *Le cycle mythologique irlandais*, which compares Irish, Greek, and Vedic myths. Joyce even mentions de Jubainville by name in the "Scylla and Charybdis" episode of *Ulysses*.[3] As Vivian Mercier indicates, the primary formal elements of *Ulysses* that derive from Homeric myth are the rhythms of search for the father, wandering, and the return home,[4] but these patterns also appear in Irish and other mythologies. Joyce's acute awareness of the episodic patterns of Irish folklore, combined with his knowledge of universal elements of folklore, allows him to create characters who may be composites of Hellenic, Hibernian, and even Hindu figures. But by identifying the thematic qualities that link them with personages from Gaelic folklore, and by examining their actions in a structural sense, we can observe the particularly Irish qualities that contribute to the Celticness in each character and episode of *Ulysses*.

LEOPOLD BLOOM, HUNGARIAN OF THE WEST

Leopold Bloom may well be the wandering hero Odysseus, who eventually is reunited with his wife, Penelope, after a series of adventures that include entrapment, challenges, and exposure to phenomena. But we may also identify him with Maelduin of the Irish *imram* or voluntary sea expedition story, a Gaelic counterpart to the Greek legend, as suggested by Stanley Sultan.[5] Sultan provides evidence of Joyce's knowledge of P. W. Joyce's *Old Celtic Romances*, in which the latter recounts "The Voyage of Maildun"; and he further establishes another connection between Bloom and Maelduin in that neither character takes revenge upon returning to a defiled home.[6] Finally, Maria Tymoczko affirms Joyce's knowledge of the romance, in that, as a regular reader of *United Irishman*, he would undoubtedly have been exposed to R. I. Best's series (appearing between October 18 and November 8, 1902), "The Old Irish Bardic Tales," which includes Imram Curaig Maele Duin (The Voyage of Mael Duin).[7] Like Maelduin, Bloom not only avoids violence and bloodshed, but tolerates and tacitly promotes his spouse's infidelity.

Bloom additionally resembles another Irish mythical character, thematically, and another source figure with whom Joyce would have been familiar. Aillil of the epic *Tain bo Cuailgne*, Medb's spouse, tolerates her affair with Fergus, recognizing that the liaison may advance Medb's cause, the acquisition of a prized bull; Bloom's wife, Molly, commits adultery with a character whom we associate with bullock features and who promotes her musical career.

But Bloom represents more than the qualities of a pre-Christian hero, for *Ulysses* contains elements of Irish Christian and pagan mythology. Though a messianic Hungarian Jew, Bloom encapsulates the traits of the folk hero of "the most belated race in Europe." He is a convert to Catholicism, like Oisin of Fenian lore, a figure Joyce would also have read about in P. W. Joyce's *Old Celtic Romances*, and, like Oisin, is never believed to have embraced the new faith. Because Bloom is not unconditionally accepted into Irish Catholic society, he shares in the alienated quality of the Irish hero. However, he demonstrates a belief in the necessity of social conventions, unlike Stephen Dedalus, who holds them in contempt, and fulfills such traditional heroic actions as attending funeral rites (in the case of Paddy Dignam) and visiting the sick and suffering (as with Mrs. Purefoy).

Bloom's empathetic gestures and sentiments are what make him, in Burgess' words, "most meet to be foster-father to a poet."[8] But if traditional Celtic heroes are generally raised by fosterers, and Stephen has already reached adulthood, it may be more appropriate to call Bloom the poet's father. It is also more logical because Stephen and Bloom are often viewed as two halves of one personality or, as Frank O'Connor explains, the subjective and objective view of the same person.[9] Bloom has objectively learned how to adjust to a world that is less than ideal, and his propensity for adaptation allies him more closely with Cuchulainn, an epic hero who accepts domestication and functions as husband and defender of his tribe from within the social sphere. The antithesis of such a personality may be found in Fionn MacCumhaill, a hero who remains a renouncer and operates from without the bounds of social structure. Bloom often receives the shabby or diffident treatment reserved for the outsider, even though he seeks acceptance from a group that rejects him (although this rejection is expressed out of earshot). The creation of such a hero calls into question the critical stance that *Ulysses*, as a novel, is a blanket condemnation of the cult of Cuchulainn.[10] While it is true that Joyce derides slavish adoration of the ancient warrior hero, Cuchulainn himself is not the target of the criticism; he views the behavior as antiprogressive and debilitating to Ireland. Joyce refrains from maintaining traditional heroic violent excess in Bloom, offering us, instead, a hero who is capable of change via integration into society. With that change comes the risk of mockery, and, like the Christ figure, Bloom is verbally crucified because of his meekness and humility.

STEPHEN DEDALUS: "A FATHER IS A NECESSARY EVIL"

Bloom's humility is not shared by Stephen Dedalus, who displays irreverence for church, homeland, and family, all three of which may be looked upon as parent symbols. "A father," Stephen said, battling against hopelessness, "is a necessary evil."[11] Having declared himself priest of artistic creation in *Portrait of the Artist*, Dedalus proceeds to practice his religion of literary endeavors. But, despite his irreverence and blasphemy, Dedalus suffers from *agenbite of inwit*, a term Joyce borrowed from the medieval catalogue of sins, *Ayenbite of Inwit*. The committal or avoidance of sin, a concept that may be a Christian adaptation of *geis* violation or recognition, pervades Irish folklore, with its mixture of magic and Christian doctrine. In "The King of Ireland's Son," a young man reaps a reward for paying the debts of a deceased man with half of his own money, thereby not violating the ancient interdiction of disrespect for the dead and gaining, as a result, not only freedom from guilt but superhuman powers. Stephen Dedalus, however, manifests more contrary thematic attributes, deliberately violating his mother's deathbed request and resultantly burdening himself with remorse. Perseverating on the oppressive influence of the Roman Catholic Church on Ireland, Dedalus exhibits an almost superstitious fear of some divine retribution or perhaps a keen remembrance of the portrait of hell painted for him at the Clongowes Wood sermon.

As a modernist, Dedalus sees the Gaelic Literary Revival as yet another negative force in Irish culture, for there is no apparent advantage to the pre-Christian alternatives. Joyce provides parody, through Stephen and friends, in "Scylla and Charybdis," mocking Yeats, Lady Gregory, Celtic lore, and occultism. Yet the indictment of "senile rural lore" is actually rendered in the form of pastiche. Stephen participates in an attack on poets and their customs that is reminiscent of *Imtheacht na Tromdhaimhe*, or *Proceedings of the Burdensome Bardic Company*. In the National Library, Stephen offers his theory of *Hamlet* as a ghost story: Shakespeare is Hamlet, and Ann Hathaway, Queen Gertrude, a subtle but significant connection to the father/son conflict of Irish folklore.

Since Bloom is associated with Hamlet, Sr. in the "Lestrygonians" episode, he and Dedalus participate in the father/son motif. And, as Stephen identifies himself with Shakespeare, as a poet, he has married his own mother. Stephen pronounces Hamnet (Shakespeare's deceased child, one of twins) a twin brother of Prince Hamlet; because Bloom, like Shakespeare, has lost a son (Rudy), Stephen, as his twin, or Prince Hamlet, becomes Bloom's own son.

This convoluted genealogy and web of identity would fit very nicely into Irish mythic family structures. Like Setanta, who "replaces" two of Dechtire's offspring, is removed from his parents and becomes Cuchulainn, Stephen Dedalus assumes the role of Bloom's dead son, forsakes his parents, and reinvents himself in his quest for a father.

Finally, Stephen Dedalus is recognizable as a Celtic hero through symbolic marks that distinguish him from other humans. He deliberately selects the ashplant, from the sacred tree of mythology, to guide him in his search for wisdom (although it could alternately become a classroom pointer, a rolled newspaper, or an umbrella). His peregrinations recall those of a scholar in a satirical Irish medieval poem of the *Book of Ballymote*, to which Joyce alludes in "Cyclops." The verse, used by

Patrick C. Power to illustrate the art of the *dinnsenchas*, or lore of high places,[12] presents a scholar who is angered because his cattle have been rustled. His wrath is ridiculed because he is ineffectual and relies upon "surgeons steel in hand that weakens."[13] No longer carrying a sword, he is symbolically impotent. Like Bloom, Stephen also wanders in a myth of topographically reduced proportions, when the geography of *Ulysses* is compared to the *Tain*, for example. The two men circuit the microcosm of mythic Ireland, but they do not bear arms; they carry a pen and walking stick.

MOLLY BLOOM: "A DROVE OF HORSES LED BY A MARE"

The principal female character of *Ulysses*, Marion Tweedy Bloom, does not undergo a single journey in the novel. She remains rooted at 7 Eccles Street, yet she travels through her memory. Molly Bloom serves as a catalyst for some of the undertakings of her husband, a quality that provides linkage to her counterparts in Irish folklore and mythology. As Bonnie Kime Scott indicates, Joyce's mythic archive is hardly limited to classical Greek models and is enriched with female figures of semidivine origin, particularly from the Irish mythological system.[14]

A composite character, Molly Bloom encompasses characteristics of Medb of the *Tain bo Cuailgne* when she issues commands to her husband and of Cuchulainn's wife, Emer, when she shows sensibility and weakness due to jealousy over her husband's presumed affair with Martha Clifford. In the *Tain*, Medb's desire for the Brown Bull of Cuailgne, which she indicates to Aillil, leads to the battles of a full-scale war; in *Ulysses*, Molly's requests for cosmetic supplies and a romantic novel are dutifully met by her husband, who undergoes interior struggles in pursuit of them. Molly has, indeed, already won her "prized bull" (Boylan), but she still enjoys being the force behind the quests of men in her life. Even while remaining in the comfort of their own beds, both Molly and the mythical Medb are capable of instigating thoughts and actions in their behalf.

Harry Levin may have been the first to observe that the course of the meanderings of *Ulysses* is "pervaded by the monthly rhythms of female nature,"[15] a theory that offers yet another parallel to the Irish epic *Tain*. Both Medb and Molly menstruate near the very end of the Ulster epic and Joyce's epic novel. Fergus has to fight a rearguard action to protect the temporarily distracted Medb; Bloom displays sensitivity to the rhythms of the female cycle, noting Gerty MacDowell's skittishness, while his wife finds them a source of distraction and irritation. In the *Tain*, Fergus grumbles: "We followed the rump of a misguided woman. It is the usual thing for a herd led by a mare to be strayed and destroyed."[16] In *Ulysses*, Bloom's erotic fantasy lingers on Molly's buttocks, and it is largely due to her voluptuousness that they remain together, in spite of her lack of constancy. A misogynistic disdain for the intellectual nature of the female combines with an appreciation for her physical attributes in both traditional works and Joyce's novel. And it is noteworthy that both the *Tain* and *Ulysses* end with a comment by or about a woman.

"TELEMACHUS": THE NEW PAGANISM

Situating the characters of *Ulysses* within episodic divisions helps us observe how Joyce employs structural devices that occur in old Irish tales. The opening scene of the first division of *Ulysses* contains a ritualistic motif that is executed by Dedalus' friend Buck Mulligan and that may signal a parody of medieval narrative structure. In "Telemachus," Mulligan performs a mock Roman Catholic mass, which action Zack Bowen suggests denotes a contemporary survival of old fertility myths of resurrection and regeneration.[17] But this action also finds its roots in the blasphemous humor of medieval Ireland. In the oldest known parody (twelfth century), *The Vision of MacConglinne*, a clerical student, Anier MacConglinne (his first name means "denier") abandons his studies for the life of a *scholaris vagans*, a wandering poet. Destined to be crucified for composing a satire on the monks of Cork, Anier has a visionary dream that enables him to cure Cathal, king of Munster, of a hunger demon and thereby be granted a stay of execution.[18] As noted in Chapter 1, Joyce has been found to mimic the alliterative and listing techniques found in this medieval work; in this instance, Mulligan makes sport of liturgical conventions and reinforces the concept that the role of the poet or artist is more prestigious than that of the cleric. Mulligan's sacrilegious performance reminds us of the sacredness of Stephen's vocation while imitating a satirical pattern of traditional Irish writing. Further, Joyce's later parody of English prose styles, in "Oxen of the Sun," a section of *Ulysses* that tends to be viewed as one that concerns itself more with experimental language than with plot, may also find its source in *The Vision of MacConglinne*, for this earlier work also parodies the literary methods used by clerical scholars.

The discourse between Stephen Dedalus and Buck Mulligan brings out conventions of folklore beyond that of parody. Mulligan calls Stephen a mummer, an expression found in folktales, especially those that call attention to costume and hair. And Dedalus, as an Irish hero, demonstrates that he has learned to despise social customs and royal authority, an accomplishment that would have taken place during the heroic education.[19] Stephen resents the "royal authority" represented by their codweller in the tower, the British Haines. In fact, "Telemachus" ends with the word "usurper," for England still dominates Hibernia, just as Haines does the tower, neither of which can be tolerable to a Gaelic hero. As a collector and compiler of "quaint" Irish folklore and a student of the Irish language, the English roommate is resented by Dedalus.

But Stephen Dedalus, through surrender of his key to Mulligan, becomes an outsider, as well, to his own domicile and, through rejection of his faith, his homeland. It is against a dual usurpation that Stephen rebels; when he calls himself the "servant of two masters," Stephen pairs British domination with the control of the patriarchal Roman Catholic Church and its papal leadership. The unwanted ecclesiastical intrusion in Irish culture, while more ancient than the British invasion, may be explored as yet another dimension of the father/son struggle with which Stephen contends. Buck Mulligan complains of his friend: "He proves by algebra that Hamlet's grandson is Shakespeare's grandfather and that he himself is the ghost of his own father."[20] Weldon Thornton remarks that he is unable to locate an interpretation of *Hamlet* as described in this passage,[21] but the significance of the friendly mockery is that it reasserts Stephen's theory of father/son reconciliation in the play. And the structural motif of generational clash, which resurfaces throughout *Ulysses*, compares to the conflict found in the *Acallamh na Senorach*.

Composed at the end of the twelfth century, age of the catastrophic Anglo-Norman invasion, the *Acallamh* was an attempt to preserve folklore at a time of usurpation. In this "Dialogue with the Elders" or "Colloquy with the Elders," the pagan Caoilte attempts to preserve Fenian lore in what Power calls "a literary expression of the confrontation between pagan and Christian Ireland," observing additionally that it is a relatively calm and peaceful piece of writing because, by the time of its composition, pagan Ireland had been "safely obliterated by generations of Christianity."[22] Joyce's character, Dedalus, a modern-age pagan, may be resuscitating a conflict between tradition and that which supplants it, via a Christian play rooted in pagan sources, Shakespeare's *Hamlet*.

To find his new order, Stephen must be set free and experience estrangement from the familiar world, a structural device that may represent an inversion of an *indarba,* or imprisonment episode. Joyce locks him out rather than sealing him in.

Stephen then hazards the inability to communicate with the human race and make himself understood. But Oisin also risks damnation when he tries to join the outsiders, the *fennidi*, in hell, and returns to Ireland, a displaced wanderer. The risks taken by both characters only affirm the extreme measures a Celtic hero will take in the advancement of his cause.

"NESTOR" AND "PROTEUS": SINNING AGAINST THE LIGHT AND "THE INELUCTABLE MODALITY OF THE VISIBLE"

Stephen Dedalus, a history teacher for pragmatic purposes, does battle in psychic wars that involve financial distress and cultural prejudices. As a literary hero, he has not been supplied with magical spears or bullets, nor has he acquired *teinm laid* or superhuman intuition. It may be true, as Declan Kiberd postulates, that Joyce deliberately avoids displays of violence in *Ulysses* to play down the image of the pugnacious Irishman.[23] Perhaps, too, Joyce refrains from writing in scenes of violence as a reaction to a world war that was going on as he composed the novel. But the encounter between Stephen Dedalus and Mr. Deasy in the "Nestor" chapter underscores the potential for altercations. The bigoted Anglo-Irish schoolmaster, a logical, thrifty conservative with reactionary political views, justifies his hatred for the Jews, explaining that they "sinned against the light," planting the seed for a later fit of violence in the young teacher's mind. Deasy, yet another usurper, recalls, with his prejudicial remark, that the expulsion of the Jews from Ireland (1290) was the result of an English movement rather than the reflection of an Irish sentiment. When Dedalus smashes a light in the brothel in the "Circe" episode, he may be displaying a delayed reaction to Deasy's words or a release of the anger and hostility that have been welling up inside him.

There is also a Celtic pagan and Christian parallel in "the

light." Cuchulainn was formerly known as Lugh, "the bright one," and the name is associated with a prototype of Fionn MacCumhaill (Fionn also meaning "light one" or "fair one"). In Christian mythology, Lucifer was once "the bright one," before he fell, while the term was later applied to a messiah. Stephen, in extinguishing the light, may be destroying both pagan and Christian symbols, freeing himself of the bondage of conformity and advancing his own alienation.

Dedalus' rejection of traditional values and his quest for truth lead him through the "Proteus" chapter, in which he reflects on the mutability of forms and their magical qualities. He assumes stronger warrior hero qualities by referring to his walking stick as an "ash sword," lending a new significance to his journey, for the truth seeker is now armed with a rapier of magical wood. Stephen at Sandymount strand looks upon the waves: "The whitemaned seahorses, champing, bright-windbridled, the steeds of Mananaan."[24] Here Joyce directly introduces the Irish sea god Mananaan MacLir, who, as Deborah Paterakis notes is as apt a source as the Hellenic god, for he, too, is a shape-changer.[25] Later, in "Scylla and Charybdis," and again in "Oxen of the Sun" and "Circe," Stephen refers to Lir, Mananaan's father, so that there can be no doubt that Joyce employs the Irish mythological figure as a symbol of metempsychosis and metamorphosis.

But MacLir's metamorphosing ability reminds Stephen of the life-robbing power of the sea, the power of the trickster, and perhaps the inherent dangers of water as symbol of the feminine. Stephen's massive urination echoes numerous Celtic folktales, in which lakes and rivers come about via this force of nature: "In long lassoes from the Cock lake the water flowed full, covering greengoldenly lagoons of sand, rising, flowing. My ashplant will float away."[26] The possible loss of Stephen's weapon, besides containing the sexual metaphor, provides a link with traditional Irish narratives, for Fergus of the Ulster Cycle, who frequently drops his sword, is understood to lose sexual prowess.

Joyce's evocation of the mutable Irish sea god and Stephen's powerlessness in controlling the cycle of tides connects to another structural   pattern from   Irish mythology. Mananaan MacLir attempted to drown the daughter borne by his wife in one of the versions of the Deirdre tales, because she was fated to bring death to two-thirds of the men of Ireland, one-third of the men of Scotland, and the three sons of Uisneach. The king's intervention stopped the drowning, and the baby grew into the beautiful woman Deirdre, who would fulfill the prophecy. (In some renditions of the Deirdre legend, she ironically drowns herself when her beloved is put to death by Conchobar.) Stephen begins his reflection in the "Proteus" episode with thoughts of midwifery, drowning, and the resignation to the idea that his existence is the fated result of a coupler's will. He observes: "From before the ages He willed me and now may not will me away or ever."[27] Euthanasia in the form of a peaceful drowning may be offered to Stephen by the god of the sea, but, like Hamlet's flood of Elsinore, the waves will not take his life. Stephen, the son, must unite with the father in consubstantiality, as must Hamlet with Hamlet, Sr.; he is not fated to drown. Moreover, suicide by immersion, which had tempted Hamlet, would represent unpardonable sin (one that haunts Bloom because of his own father's suicide), just as drowning Deirdre would have constituted *geis* violation.

Finally, Joyce imitates a motif from traditional Irish writing and its synthesis of pagan and Christian values via a crude French joke in "Proteus." When Stephen recalls the punch line "C'est le pigeon, Joseph,"[28] he refers to birdlike deities of Irish pagan and Christian belief. Deirdre is conceived by a bird; the children of Lir are turned into swans; and the Holy Ghost is represented by a dove.

"CALYPSO" AND "LOTUS EATERS":
FIRE AND WATER

Joseph Falaky Nagy informs us that fires and cooking are symbols of transition in the narratives of Irish folklore.[29] It is then appropriate that the fourth episode of *Ulysses*, which begins the second primary division of the novel, one in which we meet Leopold and Molly Bloom, start with Bloom's ritual of cooking breakfast. He also cooks in the company of a cat, possibly a Joycean substitution for the traditional canine companion of the Fenian hunter. There is, at least, a telepathic communication between human and feline in the primitive environment of the kitchen fire. Bloom's act of elimination after eating recalls an early Irish satirical piece on gluttony:

> Bit upon bit,
> Woe to him who puts them into his belly
> The Son of God will not be pleased with him
> For filling the privies.[30]

There is also a reference in a *MacConglinne* folktale to a druidic wizard's pronouncement of perfect health for one who is blessed with loose bowels. Joyce's so-called Rabelaisian humor, with its earthy overtones, stems as much from Irish tradition, in which bodily functions are openly described. Medb freely urinates on the tent floor in the *Tain*; Bloom leaves the door of the jakes ajar as he defecates; Molly adjusts herself on the commode; and Stephen urinates, as mentioned above, on the beach.

But Bloom appreciates the properties of cleansing water, contemplating a bath in a "clean trough of water, cool enamel, the gentle tepid stream,"[31] showing his enthusiasm for bathing as well as his need for baptism and communion. Though he wanders the streets of Dublin, like Stephen, without a latchkey, he does not eschew the company of others but seeks it out. Water may frighten Stephen Dedalus in its resemblance to amniotic fluid of the fetal state or its use in initiation, but Bloom finds its purifying qualities crucial.

The play of fire and water holds special meaning in traditional Irish narrative. Fionn's divine origin is said to derive from the slaying of the burner, Aillen; he tends a fire while waiting to acquire wisdom; and burning his thumb, he receives the gift of *imbas forosna*. In other renditions, Fionn is filled with knowledge directly from sacred water. Bloom's experiences with fire and water, though mundane, bear some resemblance to those of legend. He cooks and burns some inner organs (with references to searing and burnt flesh); he shows his affinity for water when he craves the refreshing qualities of the tepid bath water. Bloom visualizes himself in the liquid, combining sexual and procreative functions, but denies himself onanism for the moment. And, as the waters of baptism and rebirth are sometimes associated with drowning in Irish folklore (the ultimate resistance to conversion?), it is interesting to note that Bloom's aquatic contemplations precede his attending a funeral.

"HADES": THEN, BACK TO THE WORLD AGAIN

Leopold Bloom calls Paddy Dignam's sudden passing "the best death," but he later worries that he may simply be in a coma, hence buried alive. In this respect, Dignam assumes the qualities of the "sleeping warrior" of Fenian lore, in that the finality of his death cannot be accepted. The brief amount of time that Bloom, Power, Simon Dedalus, Cunningham, and other mourners spend at Dignam's funeral allows for comments on man's mortality and on father/son relationships, some of which remain unresolved, even after death. Cunningham agonizes over Power's denunciation of suicide because he recalls that Bloom's father had poisoned himself; Leopold mourns his deceased son, Rudy; Simon Dedalus complains about his son's choice of companions and errant ways.

The malcontent mourners reminisce about Dignam, descending, temporarily, into the paralyzed netherworld of the dead. John Riquelme observes that "Hades" is the daytime counterpart of the descent in the later "Circe" episode.[32] The chapter also seems to connect to Joyce's last tale in *Dubliners*, "The Dead," in which those who have passed on become "shades," having started to fade while they were still living, with the snow, general in Ireland, paralyzing the entire country. It is true that participating in obsequies and observing gravediggers has a numbing effect and creates a communal spirit that is not associated with other activities. But Joyce interestingly avoids implementation of the traditional Irish wake, choosing instead to introduce an episode that foreshadows the heroic entry into the Otherworld, whether it be the realm of the *sid* or a Celtic heaven or hell. For the moment, however, Joyce limits the use of this temporary paralysis to hint at otherworldly experiences, such as Bloom's reflections on love among the tombstones and will o' the wisps.

"AEOLUS" AND "LESTRYGONIANS": "I AM THY FATHER'S SPIRIT"

In addition to a parody of newspaper headlines that herald empty speeches of Irish nationalism and an indictment of the Jews, the "Aeolus" episode of *Ulysses* contains further allusions to *Hamlet*, which, though not an Irish source work, connects to some of the dilemmas that occur in Irish narratives, notably authority conflicts in parental/filial relationships and in pagan/Christian values. The identity of the father and the shift of power from father to son, along with the incest motif, are thematic and structural devices that haunt Dedalus throughout *Ulysses*.

Blaming the woman for setting things awry also appears in the "Aeolus" chapter, linking Queen Gertrude of *Hamlet*, accused by her son of incestuous acts, with Eve of Christian tradition, held responsible for the loss of Eden, as well as with other females from Irish source works. "A woman brought sin in the world. For Helen, the runaway wife of Menelaus, ten years the Greeks, O'Rourke, prince of Breffni."[33] Garrett Deasy is seen by Crawford as better off in his widowhood, having suffered for his involvement with a woman. The diminished status of notable Irishmen, from history and myth, is traced to relations with women, as in the cases of Parnell and Seymour Bushe, discussed in this chapter, and the aging Fionn MacCumhaill, who disgraces himself over Grainne. The attorney Bushe's fall from grace leads into a discussion of one of his best defenses, a fratricide case, which O'Molloy mentions to Stephen. Joyce follows with: "And in the porches of mine ear did pour."[34] Since Hamlet, Sr. was poisoned through the ear by his brother, and Stephen later explicates an intricate typological theory of King Hamlet's murder, the "poisoning of Dedalus' ear" parallels the development of his hypothesis. Stephen also ponders how King Hamlet could have known of his wife's infidelity with his brother before his own death, casting more doubts on the fidelity of the woman and recalling instances of incest in Irish legends.

Bloom, too, is caught up in the *Hamlet* conflict, serendipitously, as his thoughts wander onto King Hamlet's lines in "Lestrygonians:" "I am thy father's spirit/Doomed for a certain time to walk the earth."[35] Bloom's alliance with Stephen Dedalus is further strengthened by his own deliberate contemplation of the term *parallax*, which he links with metempsychosis. Stephen's idea of transubstantiation allows for the correspondence of historical and literary characters, and his theory of consubstantiality permits God the Father, Son, and Holy Ghost to be one. Bloom and Dedalus, therefore, translate the conflict of identifying father with son by using a literary reference, *Hamlet*. But allusions to the drama can be merely lead-ins, which cause us to work out the paternal and filial relationships from Irish tradition, or they can reaffirm that Joyce employs universal motifs from mythology and folklore, many of which display evidence of parallel development.

Bloom does specifically make reference to Irish folklore in "Lestrygonians," alluding to King Cormac, who, converted by St. Patrick, "couldn't swallow it all," [36] a terrible pun on Cormac's choking at Sletty. A twelfth-century Irish poem ("A Winter Night") recounts how Cormac MacCuileannain, king of Munster, defends his chastity from his wife by meditating on saints (such as Patrick and John) who had been delivered safe from their encounters with women. [37]

Bloom abstains from intercourse with Molly, achieves sexual gratification from Gerty MacDowell without getting near her, and derives little physical satisfaction from his relationship with Martha Clifford. Rather than reflecting on chaste saints, he tried to work out religious doctrine in general but is nonetheless saved from the taint of women. Thus the endnote of the episode for Bloom, "Safe!," albeit in reference to an errand remembered and an escape from Boylan, is also a fitting comment on the preservation of his heroic status.

"SCYLLA AND CHARYBDIS": DISPLACED MYTHS

Phillip Marcus has worked out many of the Irish allusions in *Ulysses*. He suggests that Joyce's inclusion of T. Caulfield Irwin in the catalogue of Gaelic language revivalists and occultists in the "Scylla and Charybdis" episode intensifies the bitterness of his argument with the movement, for Irwin, a Theosophist, is represented as a man who has lost his mind. [38] Distorted chronology (Joyce would have to have been ten when he met Irwin, according to the text) may fulfill the same function as the displacement of characters and the general theme of madness, as it relates to *Hamlet*. Joyce, alluding to Douglas Hyde's *Love Songs of Connaught*, may be saying that the Gaelic revivalists' obsession with folklore and their interest in associating countless Irish landmarks with ancient Irish legends is not unlike the monomaniacal focus of Prince Hamlet. It is also ironic that Dedalus' British codweller Haines, who has studied the Gaelic language, is purchasing a copy of Hyde's work.

Stephen, like Hamlet, has his own ghost to contend with, the specter of his heritage, but, like Shakespeare's character, he also sees that the discovery of some truth compels action. The promoters of inflated myths instigate complications, too, in their celebration of Irish culture: "People do not know how dangerous love songs can be, the auric egg of Russell warned occultly. The movements which work revolutions in the world are born out of the dreams and visions in a peasant's heart on the hillside. For them the earth is not an exploitable ground but the living mother."[39] Once a spirit of chauvinism has been aroused, action must be taken against the oppressor. Æ may be associating the earth-mother with the goddess Danaan, as Weldon Thornton explains,[40] but the reference is vital because the matriarchal figure traditionally spurs on revolution. Hamlet's predicament, too, is largely brought about by his mother's doings and resultant confusion.

Connections with Shakespeare continually take us back to Irish sources. R. I. Best, translator of de Jubainville's *Irish Mythological Cycle*, points out that the "brother motive" is found in old Irish myths; Stephen Dedalus mentions that the underplot of *King Lear*, in which Edmund figures, is taken from Sidney's *Arcadia* and tacked onto a Celtic legend older than history. The validation of Irish sources in this episode makes it clear that Joyce does not lampoon the legends themselves. Yeats, Synge, and Lady Gregory, objects of blatant satire, are probably found guilty of trying to rewrite or dramatize these tales in a literal or formal way.

Joyce prefers a multilayered approach to the use of folklore motifs, in the tradition of *Hamlet* and *King Lear*. Mananaan MacLir is invoked by a druid to drown the adulterous lovers,

Deirdre and Naoise; Hamlet would rather see his mother dead than living in sin with Claudius; and Stephen appeals to the sea god to drown the prostitutors of "virgin Dublin."

"WANDERING ROCKS" AND "SIRENS": PRESERVATION AND DESTRUCTION

In the nineteen divisions of "Wandering Rocks," an episode with no thematic parallel episode in the *Odyssey*, we can observe a few motifs from Irish folklore. Lady Belvedere's *Hamlet*/incest allusion in her reflections on infidelity with her husband's brother can be compared to the mythic Irish Cuchulainn's mother, who has an incestuous relationship with her own brother, Conchobar, although what is tolerated in the mythic character may not be as acceptable in ordinary mortals.

Stephen Dedalus' sister's irreverent remark, "Our father who art not in heaven" (a reference to Simon Dedalus) is inserted in the chapter after a description of Father Conmee's daily rounds. The priest's reflections on "that tyrannous incontinence" necessary for the proliferation of the human race takes us back to blasphemous Mulligan and traditional Irish mockery of the clergy in medieval writings, although the satirist usually retracted his criticism to some degree. As David Krause tells us, rebellion against the clergy really mirrors the tragicomic conflict between father and son in Irish myth and legend.[41]

Another element from Irish folklore, thematic in nature, may be seen in Joyce's redefining the Celtic hero, a concept he develops more fully in a later episode. Lenehan praises Tom Rochford for his manhole rescue ("a heroic act"), juxtaposing the risks of exposure to sewer gases with the dangers traditionally encountered by the warrior hero. And Haines identifies Stephen with a hero from mythology after Buck Mulligan calls him "a wandering Aengus," a god of love and beauty. Stephen's comrades mock him as one who can find no proof of the existence of hell in Irish myth; as a *fili*/poet, they prophesy that he will compose "something" in ten years, marginalizing the function of the bard.

Other thematic motifs from Irish traditional narratives appear in the musical motif of the "Sirens" episode. The sound of the sirens, deadly in Greek mythology, carries the same danger in Irish lore. Female trickster figures, the Celtic *merrows*, lead sailors to the green grave, a notion that bears out the misogynistic conception of the female in much Irish writing. Surrender to feminine wiles, whether displayed by literal or metaphorical sirens, reduces heroic status and leads to misfortune. Thus the "harmless" flirtations of Miss Douce and Miss Kennedy belie their true nature; indeed, they ridicule Bloom when he is not present. The barmaids at the Ormond Hotel establish an atmosphere in which the drinkers feel comfortable discussing Molly Bloom lasciviously, and it is not coincidental that she is having a rendezvous with Boylan at this hour. Bloom escapes entrapment by the females in "Sirens," recognizing the ills they portend, even if only subliminally, for he studies the mermaid poster on the door before exiting.

"CYCLOPS": REDUCING THE IRISH HERO

Inflated heroism, puffing of numbers, and endless catalogues are all subject to satire in the "Cyclops" episode of *Ulysses*. Joyce draws from the poetry of Donald MacConsidine, a source for Douglas Hyde's *Love Songs of Connaught*, for the impressive Gaelic recitation of the citizen's dog, Garryowen. Joyce points out, in mock elucidation, that Garryowen, who communicates in Gaelic with his master (whose name is intentionally written with a lowercase "c"), recites a poem that illustrates an Irish *rann*, an embellishment found in traditional Irish poetry.

This decorative device is said to be lost in the translation of the poem into English, just as the Irish hero, we may presume, has been somewhat lost in the portrayals found in nineteenth-century translations of Irish epics. In one of the sharpest cynical passages of the entire novel, Joyce describes the citizen as a man who is a "broad-shouldered deepchested stronglimbed frankeyed redhaired freely freckled shaggybearded wide-mouthed largenosed longheaded deepvoiced barekneed brawnyhanded hairylegged ruddyfaced sinewyarmed hero."[42] A composite of all Irish stereotypes, heroic and nonheroic, the description leads to a massive list of heroic figures, beginning with Cuchulainn, and imitates the recitation of genealogies undertaken by the *dinnsenchas* poets. Joyce mocks the epic technique via inclusion of such names as Lady Godiva and Herodotus, a strategy he appears to fancy when he constructs a list of wedding guests, Irish monuments, and saints and monks, eventually reducing the convention to farcical proportions.

More important than the pastiche of storytelling techniques in this chapter is the intrusion of the first actual narrative persona, as Karen Lawrence notes.[43] The disagreeable narrator becomes a comic *seanachie* in his encyclopedic recitation of lists in the biblical/Gaelic tradition. He invents the twelve tribes of Ireland, which would unite Bloom, as descendant of the lost tribes of Israel, with the Celtic hero: "And there sat with him the high sinhedrim of the twelve tribes of Iar, for every tribe one man, of the tribe of Patrick and of the tribe of Hugh and of the tribe of Owen and of the tribe of Conn and of the tribe of Oscar and of the tribe of Fergus and of the tribe of Finn and of the tribe of Dermot and of the tribe of Cormac and of the tribe of Kevin and of the tribe of Caolte and of the tribe of Ossian, there being in all twelve good men and true."[44] Such an assemblage of saints and heroes represents a synthesis of the sacred and the secular, for Joyce alludes to the twelve apostles of the New Testament and the twelve members of a jury, a structural element he will recreate in *Finnegans Wake*.

In the meantime, if Bloom is to be evaluated and judged as a true Gaelic hero, it is interesting that the judgment will come from the crude and bigoted citizen, who ridicules him and calls him "the new Messiah for Ireland Island of saints and sages!"[45] Perhaps Joyce asserts here that the ordinary Irish citizen is incapable of recognizing a saint or a hero, in light of the overstated portraits depicted by liturgical literature and hero sagas of the revivalists. And the noble features of the canine, who normally carries no absurd connotations in Celtic traditional narrative,[46] are so inflated as to make him appear ridiculous. The feisty setter, an animal Stephen phobically fears, is the source of his master's boastfulness, thereby contributing to the reduction of the Irish hero and preparing for the development of a new model for heroism.

"NAUSICAA" AND "OXEN OF THE SUN": PROCREATIVE ACTS

Hugh Kenner observes that many climaxes in *Ulysses*, such as Molly and Blazes' trysting hour, occur offstage, in the Greek tradition.[47] But others, of both a sexual and nonsexual nature, are achieved before the reader's eyes. When Bloom experiences orgasm in the "Nausicaa" episode of *Ulysses*, the source of his pleasure is a girl who is "Greekly perfect," yet "a specimen of winsome Irish girlhood," Gerty MacDowell. Again we see the fusion of mythologies and the immediacy of Irish motifs.

It is not unusual for the Celtic hero to experience, in his travels, sexual fulfillment with or by women other than his spouse or bride-to-be. Cuchulainn has liaisons with Uathach and Aife, begetting a son by the latter, but these affairs do not diminish his love for Emer. In the case of literary Bloom, as Burgess explains, all women lead home to one—Molly.[48] And, while Gerty MacDowell is neither as forward nor as beautiful as the legendary, seductive Deirdre (she is, in fact, handicapped), she is aware of her best features and takes pleasure in her ability to tantalize: "Gerty just took off her hat for a moment to settle her hair and a prettier, daintier head of nutbrown tresses was never seen on a girl's shoulders—a radiant

little vision, in sooth, almost maddening at the sweetness."[49]
Bloom's act of onanism on Sandymount Shore provides guilt-
free satisfaction and protects him from temptation that will
plague him later in "Circe." Unlike Cormac, he will not have
to pray to the saints for chastity, for his seed will have been
spent.

Bloom is further linked with Stephen on the strand where
the young poet contemplated union and mortality, thanking
Gerty "for this relief," then remembering that the quotation
comes from *Hamlet*, a source of fixation for Dedalus. And, if
there is a sublimated sentiment of incestuously derived arousal
by the girl/woman MacDowell, who may represent Bloom's
own daughter Milly, then the quotation from *Hamlet* is a fitting reminder of the incest motif. As mentioned earlier, themes
of incest are often treated dispassionately in Irish folklore. In
the tale of Clothru, a young girl sleeps with her three brothers,
who are planning to kill their parents, in the hopes that a child
will be conceived, so that some good might come of the act.[50]
This extreme example from a culture that rejoices in fertility
above all else, even within an incestuous union, would absolve
Bloom of any guilt over his prurient interest in the young
woman.

The sacredness of fertility in Irish traditional narratives is
highlighted again in the following episode, "Oxen of the Sun."
Joyce again imitates the structural invocation of the *Vision of
MacConglinne*, beginning with a Latin, Celtic, and English
chant; then he proceeds to imitate English prose styles from
the Anglo-Saxon period to the nineteenth century. But this
episode unites *Ulysses* with Irish folklore most strongly in its
focus on procreation. The cow, a symbol of fertility, figures
prominently in the titles of tales of Cuchulainn's boyhood
deeds, *Lebor na Huidre* or *The Book of the Dun Cow*, in the epic
Tain bo Cuailgne, or *Cattle Raid of Cooley*, and in recordings of
dialogues between Deirdre and Naoise, in which she calls him a
young bull whom she would take any day over the bull of the

province (Conchobar). Obviously, both genders of the bovine species are required to ensure proliferation.

While attending the birth of Mrs. Purefoy's son, Bloom is appalled at the mention of Mr. Deasy's newspaper article on hoof and mouth disease, calling for a mass slaughter of the infected animals. Dixon's rejoinder leads into a discussion of bulls and male sexual prowess as they await news on the progress of maternity. Mrs. Purefoy, having spent three days in labor, is portrayed as a fecund bovine about to calve. The notion of sacrificing her unborn child to save her own life, a sin in Catholic doctrine, is also compared to the cow's act of consuming the tender newborn calf, perhaps an analogy to Ireland, which is sometimes bitterly represented as the sow that eats her own farrow. Such a sacrifice, to Bloom, would also be the equivalent of ideating on an unworthy figure, anticipating pleasure without the reward. Barren results would preclude closure and disrupt the cycle of fertility.

Unfortunately, Haines' intrusion in Holles Street Hospital and his pronouncment, "The vendetta of Mananaan!," reminds us that the progeny will eventually overcome and replace the progenitor. And, carrying a portfolio of Celtic literature in one hand and a vial marked "Poison" in the other, Haines reminds Stephen Dedalus that his curse is the assumption of the role of his father. Mongan, a rebirth of the sea god, Mananaan, receives a visit from his father as a ghost, just as Prince Hamlet meets Hamlet, Sr. in spectral form; and, one day, Stephen will assume the role of the biological father he has renounced. The joy of Mrs. Purefoy's delivery will be offset when the child becomes the parent; the allusion to Mananaan and the metempsychosis found in Irish mythology bring Bloom back in memory to earlier days when he, too, had a son.

"CIRCE": MORE SHAPE-CHANGERS

Joyce may have borrowed Circean motifs from Homer and portions of Goethe's "Walpurgisnacht," as well as Sacher von

Masoch's *Venus in Furs*, but he also uses numerous Irish folk-lore motifs in this division. Humans and animals undergo lit-eral metamorphosis; the incest motif is repeated; interdictions or *geasa* come to light; early Irish Sheela-na-gig imagery ap-pears; and Mananaan MacLir resurfaces. And, as Riquelme says, because language lacks denotative limits in this fantastic mid-night episode, meaning becomes connotative.[51] Thus language may have little to do with plot and much to do with underly-ing influences. "Circe" resembles a Celtic *bruidhean* tale in that Bloom and Stephen are lured to and almost forcibly contained in a brothel in which they are subjected to magical interfer-ences (even if the occurrences are the products of their own imaginations). In the realistic portions of the episode, such as Stephen's fracas with Privates Compton and Carr, and Ste-phen's breaking of the chandelier, Bloom assumes a mentor or helper role, not unlike that of a Celtic *ceadach*, for he tries to protect Stephen from his own excessive behavior. But Bloom is also tempted and tried for the excesses in his own personality.

As the "new womanly man," Bloom could possibly become pregnant, a structural motif that is not alien to traditional Irish narratives. In Fenian lore, a warrior in "The Feast of Congal" metamorphoses sexually every other year, bearing children when he is a woman. "Dr." Mulligan's pronouncement of Bloom as *virgo intacta* may also be related to an Irish folktale, "The Romance of Mis and Dubh Ruis." In the folklore, a young woman, Mis, possibly drawn from a goddess of the Mythological Cycle, regains her virginity after repeated sexual experiences.[52]

Bloom undergoes more torture, even though he masochisti-cally appears to enjoy it. He crumbles when reminded of his many sins of omission or commission, from soiling his trou-sers (violating a mother's interdiction) to entering a brothel, masturbating, and allowing himself to entertain incestuous thoughts of his daughter Milly (violating church law). Stephen, too, confronts another specter of his mother, who reminds him of her unfulfilled request, though he belligerently maintains his Ossianic *non-serviam* attitude and with it his abiding guilt. Stephen continues to quote from *Hamlet*, unable to abandon his search for a father, even stating that he was born "Thursday. Today," hence newborn in the fantasy.

Zoe, the prostitute, is not unlike the hag precursor of the Sheela-na-gig goddess of creation and destruction; and Bella/Bello Cohen fills the role of yet another witchlike shapechanger, who satisfies Bloom's masochistic needs. Metamorphosis, fundamental to Irish traditional writings, achieves its peak when the citizen's dog, Garryowen, reappears as the ghost of Paddy Dignam, and, in the tradition of *Richard III*, a parade of ghosts sweeps through the fantasy, including that of Bloom's father, Virag his son, Rudy, and the voices of souls from heaven and hell. Mananaan MacLir enters, invoking the alchemist Hermes Trismegistos, then fittingly changes form. Finally, Bloom sees the face of his dead son, restoring a touch of reality to the episode and drawing Bloom closer to Stephen.

"EUMAEUS" AND "ITHACA": EDUCATION

Bloom's position as helper figure with Stephen solidifies in the "Eumaeus" and "Ithaca" divisions of *Ulysses*. Bloom, ultimately a pragmatic and commercially-oriented individual, pales alongside Stephen as a warrior hero, yet he qualifies as educator because he transfers the hero spatially, albeit not magically, away from the chaotic brothel and, eventually, to his own home. Stephen's disoriented wanderings expose him to other tricksters, like the braggart sailor, W. B. Murphy. The maritime windbag, as *miles gloriosus*, expands his tall tales as the audience eggs him on, affording Joyce another opportunity to satirize Yeats' renditions of Irish mythological and folktales. Stephen becomes a spectator to ritualistic conversations of the male tribe. The discussion of Parnell's career, ruined through his indiscretion with a married woman, Kitty O'Shea (whom Bloom mentally connects with his own unfaithful spouse), recalls the Gaelic traditional belief in death or dishonor via association with a woman. While Cumhaill of Fenian lore literally died when he married, Parnell's untimely demise is blamed on the interference of a woman in his life: "She put the first nail in his coffin."[53]

Stephen's education continues in the "Ithaca" episode. Karen Lawrence remarks on a sense of "displacement" in this chapter, as though one story were being recorded as another takes place.[54] But this format recalls the ritualistic training of the Irish hero; the question-answer plan imitates the precision of the *fili* or poet's education, in which imitation, rote learning, and practice produce technique. Similarly, traditional Roman Catholic catechism learning occurs through repetition and continual advancement to the next topic. While these parodied rote devices obviously do aid the memory, Joyce explores more connections between ancient and modern, pagan and Christian literature through their strategies of memorization. It is noteworthy, too, that one of the first topics that Bloom and Stephen discuss is the Christian conversion of Ireland.

Joyce parodies the rituals of education in action as well as in form in "Ithaca." Bloom's rite of cocoa preparation resembles that of the Roman Catholic mass and other initiatory ceremonies. Finally, Stephen and Bloom are spatially united within the stylized episode, though whether Stephen actually receives or accepts illuminating knowledge is not to be ascertained.

As Joyce has created an Irish urban folktale, with a mélange of motifs from mythology and folklore, it is tempting to force closure upon the epic work and suggest that the young hero has found enlightenment. But it appears that a tacit union of father and son has been reached, one that is best observed in their silence: "each contemplating the other in both mirrors of the reciprocal flesh of theirhisnothis fellowfaces."[55]

"PENELOPE": "A WOMAN IS SO SENSITIVE ABOUT EVERYTHING"

Molly Bloom's interior monologue, a lengthy addendum to the action of *Ulysses*, provides a logical conclusion to the work. It reminds us that a feminine point of view will be the last one the reader retains, just as the audience of the epic *Tain* is left with the memory of Medb's incapacity and its effect on one of the last major battles of the raid. Molly's thoughts also reinforce the idea that a female has entered the minds and discussions of many characters in *Ulysses* and dominated the thoughts of her husband. Like Medb, she has wielded a great deal of power.

But Molly is a kindred spirit to more than one female of Irish narrative tradition. She embodies many of the qualities of several female heroines, as well as universal qualities found in heroines of other cultures. She is unabashed about her physical needs and desires and expresses this freely: "I suppose thats what a woman is supposed to be there for or He wouldnt have made us the way He did so attractive to men."[56] Such a lack of inhibition can be found in Deirdre, who, prior to her marriage to the aging Conchobar, tells Naoise that she would readily take a young bull like him. The "emancipated" heroine also occurs in Emer, who denies Cuchulainn "a sweet country," her breasts, until he has performed acts of bravery for her. As Edna O'Brien explains in her famous essay, "Why Irish Heroines Don't Have to Be Good Anymore," the prototypes of many literary characters are goddesses or goddesslike women who assert themselves sexually and socially.

Molly Bloom displays such a confidence, teasing Mulvey when she reflects on refusing him sexual intercourse (out of fear of pregnancy), yet participating in other sexual activities with him. Because of her uninhibited nature, Molly enjoys her physicality without restraint. But this feature of her personality leads to narcissism. As the curvaceous and voluptuous female, Molly exhibits some of the grotesqueness of the Irish

Sheela-na-gig, the earthmother goddess: "my belly is a bit too big. Ill have to knock off the stout at dinner or am I getting too fond of it."[57] Her exaggerated descriptions of the erotic/maternal features of her body, such as mother's milk "sweeter and thicker than cow's milk," are rapidly associated with sexual play: "he wanted to milk me into the tea,"[58] reaffirming that in *Ulysses*, as in traditional Irish writings, lust and procreation are never far apart.

Molly also introduces imagery reminiscent of the Irish phallic father-god, Dagda, in her description of Blazes Boylan. The primitive and occasionally vulgar nature of Molly's thoughts link her with some of the earlier Irish tales that had not undergone Lady Gregory's editing. But the temptress image of Molly Bloom is not very far removed, at times, from the immoral characterization assigned to Medb by medieval monastics. Joyce reminds us that Molly is metaphorically (as a temptress) and literally (as a singer) a siren: "if I can only get in with a handsome young poet at my age."[59] Molly the seducer wishes to be immortalized in the poet's writing, then acknowledges that the poet himself would not fit into her life. She cruelly derides her husband: "its a wonder Im not an old shrivelled hag before my time living with him so cold."[60] And her views on adultery absolve Bloom and her of any guilt and recall the licentious behavior found in many Irish folktales: "if thats all we ever did in this vale of tears God knows its not much doesnt everybody only they hide it."[61]

If Joyce seeks to maintain the tradition of portraying the woman as a threat to the hero's honor and as domesticator of the warrior, then he does so with reservation in Molly Bloom. She balances Stephen's struggle with Catholicism and national identity and Bloom's fear of sin with a total acceptance of both the pagan and Christian sides of her nature. Molly reads the cards and goes to confession. Her pantheistic adoration of roses, jessamines, geraniums, and cactuses and her admiration of nature in general may be likened to her indictment of atheism and her conviction in the existence of a supreme being. Joyce's decision to close *Ulysses* with a sensory appeal to perfumed gardens and Molly's perfumed breasts recalls the significance of the physical beauty in Irish mythological and folktale sources. Yet Molly's affirmation of Christian values, with many references to God, informs us that she acknowledges the sensuality of the scene, yet recognizes the supernatural force behind its creation.

NOTES

1. Zack Bowen, "*Ulysses*," in *A Companion to Joyce Studies*, eds. Zack Bowen and James Carens (Westport, Conn.: Greenwood Press, 1984), p. 432.

2. Anthony Burgess, *ReJoyce* (New York: W. W. Norton and Co., 1965), p. 33.

3. James Joyce, *Ulysses*, ed. Hans Walter Gabler (New York: Garland, 1981), p. 399. All references to *Ulysses* are from this edition.

4. Vivian Mercier, *The Irish Comic Tradition* (Oxford: Oxford University Press, 1962), p. 213.

5. Stanley Sultan, "An Old Irish Model for *Ulysses*," *James Joyce Quarterly* 5 (1968), p. 105.

6. Ibid., p. 107.

7. Maria Tymoczko, *The Irish Ulysses* (Berkeley: University of California Press, 1994), p. 185.

8. Burgess, *ReJoyce* (New York: W.W. Norton and Co., Inc., 1965), p. 109.

9. Frank O'Connor, *A Short History of Irish Literature* (New York: G.P. Putnam's Sons, 1967), p. 202.

10. Declan Kiberd, "The Vulgarity of Heroics," in *James Joyce: An International Perspective*, eds. Suheil Badi Bushrui and Bernard Benstock (Totowa, N. J.: Barnes and Noble, 1982), p. 158.

11. *Ulysses*, p. 443.

12. Patrick C. Power, *A Literary History of Ireland* (Cork: Mercier Press, 1969), p. 31.

13. Ibid.

14. Bonnie Kime Scott, *James Joyce* (Atlantic Highlands, N. J.: Humanities Press International, 1987), p. 79.

15. Harry Levin, *James Joyce: A Critical Introduction* (Norfolk, Va.: New Directions, 1941), p. 125.

16. Thomas Kinsella, trans., *Tain bo Cuailgne* (Oxford: Oxford University Press, 1970), p. 251.

17. Zack Bowen, *Ulysses as a Comic Novel* (Syracuse: Syracuse University Press, 1989), p. 20.

18. Kuno Meyer, ed. and trans., *The Vision of MacConglinne: A Middle Irish Wonder Tale* (1892; rpt. New York: Lemma Publishing Corp., 1974), p. 30.

19. Marie-Louise Sjoestedt-Jonval, *Dieux et héros des celtes* (Paris: Presses universitaires de France, 1940), p. 87.

20. *Ulysses*, p. 33.

21. Weldon Thornton, *Allusions in Ulysses* (Chapel Hill: University of North Carolina Press, 1962), p. 23.

22. Powers, *A Literary History of Ireland*, p. 40.

23. Kiberd, "The Vulgarity of Heroics," p. 158.

24. *Ulysses*, p. 77.

25. Deborah T. Paterakis, "Mananaan MacLir in *Ulysses*," *Éire/Ireland* 7, no. 3 (1972), p. 32.

26. *Ulysses* , p. 101.

27. Ibid., p. 77.

28. Ibid., p. 28.

29. Joseph Falaky Nagy, *The Wisdom of the Outlaw* (Berkeley: University of California Press, 1985), p. 168.

30. Mercier, *The Irish Comic Tradition*, p. 124.

31. *Ulysses*, p. 175.

32. John Riquelme, *Teller and Tale in Joyce's Fiction* (Baltimore: Johns Hopkins University Press, 1983), p. 168.

33. *Ulysses*, p. 275.

34. Ibid., p. 291.

35. Ibid., p. 321.

36. Ibid., p. 357.

37. O'Connor, *A Short History of Irish Literature*, p. 80.

38. Phillip Marcus, "Notes on Irish Elements in 'Scylla and Charybdis,'" *James Joyce Quarterly* 10 (1973), p. 318.

39. *Ulysses*, p. 399.

40. Thornton, *Allusions in Ulysses*, p. 158.

41. David Krause, *The Profane Book of Irish Comedy* (Ithaca, N.Y.: Cornell University Press, 1982), p. 64.

42. *Ulysses*, p. 639.

43. Karen Lawrence, *The Odyssey of Style in Ulysses* (Princeton: Princeton University Press, 1981), p. 101.

44. *Ulysses*, pp. 696-697.

45. Ibid., p. 725.

46. James MacKillop, *Fionn MacCumhaill: Celtic Myth in English Literature* (Syracuse: Syracuse University Press, 1986), p. 49.

47. Hugh Kenner, *Joyce's Voices* (Berkeley: University of California Press, 1978), p. 42.

48. Burgess, *ReJoyce*, p. 149.

49. *Ulysses*, p. 775.

50. O'Connor, *A Short History of Irish Literature*, p. 45.

51. Riquelme, *Teller and Tale in Joyce's Fiction*, p. 139.

52. Mercier, *The Irish Comic Tradition*, p. 42.

53. *Ulysses*, p. 1421.

54. Lawrence, *The Odyssey of Style in Ulysses*, p. 182.

55. Ibid., p. 1549.

56. Ibid., p. 1723.

57. Ibid., p. 1661.

58. Ibid., p. 1669.

59. Ibid., p. 1713.

60. Ibid., p. 1715.

61. Ibid., p. 1723.

CHAPTER 3

Finnegans Wake: Imitating Sources

James Joyce's use of mythological allusions, both Hibernian and Hellenic, is primarily intellectual, literal, historical, or satirical in *Ulysses* because most of the action occurs in the waking state. The episodes that prove exceptions to this rule, "Hades" and "Circe," are structurally and thematically closest to myth because they deal with descents into the realm of the dead or into the world of the unconscious. Thus devices such as the integration of Christian elements in pagan Celtic netherworlds and the tradition of metamorphosis are restricted to those episodes that are temporarily removed from the conscious state. Joyce, the modern storyteller, subtly weaves elements of Irish mythological and folktale sources in a largely realistic novel. The fantastical possibilities of Irish mythology are not yet fully developed.

In *Finnegans Wake* (1939), which follows *Ulysses* after a seventeen-year interval, Joyce not only reiterates the mythic themes of his earlier work; he makes them the focus of the novel and patterns them after recognizable Irish folktales. Because *Finnegans Wake* may largely be read as a dream, and the dream state is closer to the collective unconscious and more primitive in nature, the work may be closely allied with myth.

Devices that occur in Celtic lore and are introduced in *Ulysses*
appear in a more overt manner in *Finnegans Wake*. Also, as
Finnegans Wake is meant to be read aloud, it is closer to oral
tradition, even though the Letter, which derives from written-
tradition, creates multiple readings. This oral/visual strategy
may represent an experimental adaptation of the Gaelic *seanachie*/storyteller tradition in the modern novel.

Because so many features of traditional Gaelic writings are
found in this epic novel, I focus here on how they ally Joyce's
work with early sources. When the shape-changers of the
"Proteus" episode of *Ulysses* resurface in *Finnegans Wake*, it is
not with the randomness of the mutating sea god. When Shem
and Shaun metamorphose into animal, vegetable, mineral, and
spatial forms, their fusion contributes to the father/son conflict of traditional Irish works. Youth (Shem/Shaun) murders
old age (HCE), but, in the course of the rebellion, Joyce refers
frequently to St. Patrick and his argument with Oisin.

The patricide is partly caused by *geis* violation or the breaking of some moral code in *Finnegans Wake*. While this novel
reinforces the concept of the importance of adherence to the
hero's injunctions and respect for interdictions, it connects
modern literature more closely with Irish folktales, for the
breaker of *geis* is shown not only to diminish in stature but to
undergo execution. Stephen Dedalus' remorse in *Ulysses* contributes to a sort of self-flagellation, through *agenbite of inwit*;
HCE's misdeed in *Finnegans Wake* results in trial and physical
punishment when he is metamorphosed as the Russian General.

Another pattern of Irish mythology that is touched on in
Ulysses and becomes a central feature of *Finnegans Wake* is the
presentation of several versions of one incident or story. While
not only one version may be completely true or factual, there
will be thematic and structural similarities among them. When
Leopold and Molly Bloom ruminate on Molly's alleged liaisons in *Ulysses*, the reader is never certain that any extramarital

sexual encounter actually took place except that with Blazes Boylan; in the urban folktale, there is no empirical evidence of Molly's multiple affairs. Likewise, the various renditions of the infamous Letter of *Finnegans Wake* demonstrate how Irish folktales undergo constant change. The medieval and later chroniclers of Irish folklore and history, whether monastic or scholastic, each contributed his own touch to the individual recording, as do the composers and analysts of the Letter in *Finnegans Wake*.

Finally, Joyce constructs modern myth via a process that resembles transliteration, as he blends Christian and pagan elements in his novels. There is perhaps no other mythological system like that of the Celts, which so readily assimilated Catholic values into its pre-Christian tales. Bloom's spirit of ecumenism in *Ulysses* extends to HCE's identification with the pagan Fionn MacCumhaill and a newly crowned pope in *Finnegans Wake*. And one of the best means of expressing the link between pagan and Christian values is the employment of numerological devices. Joyce synthesizes the Celtic triad and the Christian trinity in his second epic novel, just as postconversion folktales assigned Christlike attributes to Cuchulainn.

All of the patterns of Gaelic folklore that occur in *Finnegans Wake* are interrelated and may be discussed within the context of medieval writings. The use of metamorphosis and role confusion allows for a reenactment of the Dialogues with St. Patrick; *geis* violation prompts Ossianic rebellion, whether of the sons against the father or of one son against the other; plot repetition recalls the difficulty of preserving Irish folktales as closely as possible to their original version; and numerological devices underscore the fluidity of the transition of pagan folklore to Christianized folklore.

METAMORPHOSIS AND ROLE CONFUSION:
A NEW *ACCALAMH NA SENORACH*

In Irish legends, complete or partial metamorphosis often serves the purpose of deception or defense. In the Fenian Cycle, Saba, Oisin's mother, is turned into a deer by a jealous druid so that Fionn can never find her again. Cuchulainn's grotesque physical distortions, while one of his peculiarities, also serves the metamorphic purpose of protecting him in battle by increasing his prowess and frightening the enemy. In Joyce's novels, change of shape or appearance allows for a merging of all these purposes. When a character alters form, he is either immune to physical harm, defending himself from the enemy without, or to psychological harm, which may come from the enemy within. Thus metamorphosis provides for both protection and self-deception. Only the listener or reader may recognize the metamorphosed character (albeit with difficulty at times, in *Finnegans Wake*), just as the listener to the Gaelic storyteller once knew the hero in disguise and understood his need for camouflage.

While it is true that shape-changing allows us to identify HCE of *Finnegans Wake* with numerous mythological, folktale, literary, and historical figures, it is especially significant that he appears as the legendary Finn MacCool (Fionn Mac-Cumhaill in a deliberately popularized Anglicized orthographic choice), a prominent character from indigenous Irish folklore and Irish culture. James MacKillop is correct when he asserts that there is no apparent continuity in the order of references to Fionn MacCumhaill in the text, and he goes on to trace the development of a Fenian motif in the thirteen-page riddle of Book One, Chapter Six (whose answer is "Finn") and in the later pages of Book Two, Chapter Three, which treat heroism and the Diarmaid and Grainne legend.[1] The ostensible randomness of allusions to Fionn suits the structure of *Finnegans Wake* as an Ossianic text. It is more likely that the ongoing struggle against authority and fear of *geis* or sin, two major themes of the novel, are traceable to the traditional *Acallamh na Senorach*, if we view the sporadic references to Fionn as clues to the imitative nature of the novel. Just as one purpose of the medieval *Acallamh* was to preserve the tradition of peasant folklore, so *Finnegans Wake*, in both passing references to and intensive treatment of Fenian legend, continues the preservation.

The story of the *Acallamh*, also known as the *Colloquy with the Elders* and *Dialogues with St. Patrick*, initially relates how two members of Fionn's tribe, the *fianna*, survived the general slaughter of the Battle of Gabhra and met at Drogheda one hundred and fifty years later. Oisin, Fionn's son, went north to visit his mother; Caoilte, Fionn's nephew, remained with St. Patrick, and the two went around Ireland. Oisin did not meet the saint until later in the story, at which time he recounted the deeds of Fionn and the *fennidi*, which were duly recorded by a *seanachie*.[2] It is in the later, Renaissance renditions of the *Acallamh* that the emphasis is placed on Oisin's resistance to St. Patrick's conversion attempts, and farcical elements are stressed in the tale. But in the earliest recorded version, Caoilte associates Gaelic lore with geography in the manner of the *dinnsenchas*, while the Christian saint counters with stories about Christianity. Thus a second purpose of the *Acallamh*, that of permitting the sacred and profane to coexist peacefully, is repeated in *Finnegans Wake*, which blends elements of pagan (Fenian) and Christian (New Testament) traditions.

Humphrey Chimpden Earwicker, the publican, must therefore be tried as a deceased Christian man and as a pagan sleeping warrior in the course of the topographically inspired narration of Irish folklore in order for all of the elements of the Ossianic *Acallamh* to be present in *Finnegans Wake*. As will be seen, Joyce effects this largely through his use of metamorphosis. HCE/Fionn is discussed as the subject of the first riddle in Book One, Chapter Six; "Shaun MacIrewick" (son of Earwicker), briefdragger (letter carrier) assumes the role of the enemy and prosecutor; and "twelve apostrophes" (twelve apostles or twelve elders of the Colloquy) sit in judgment. HCE's son, "Shaun the Postman," may be allied with Fionn's enemy, Goll MacMorna, as suggested by MacKillop,[3] but it is more likely that he represents the *seanachie* or recorder of the question/answer procedure: "He misunderstruck an aim for am ollo of number three of them and left his free natural ripostes to four of them in their own fine artful disorder."[4] The role of Oisin, which Adaline Glasheen assigns to Earwicker's son Shem in her exhaustive study of the metamorphoses of *Finnegans Wake*, in "Who Is Who When Everybody Is Somebody Else,"[5] is that of the recounter of HCE/Fionn's exploits in response to geographical memory triggers. And the Ossianic structure of Chapter Six and Shem the Penman's defense are clearly introduced at the end of Book One, Chapter Five: "Howbeit we heard not a son of sons to leave by him to oceanic society in his old man without a thing in his ignorance, Tulko MacHooley."[6]

The glorification of Fenian folktales begins as Dublin, the River Liffey, and HCE's daily path are employed as were the loci of adventures retold in the *Acallamh*. "His birth proved accidental shows his death a grave mistake"[7] allies HCE with Fionn, as one marked by unusual birth and untouched by death. As a *gilla* or youth, HCE went "nudiboots with trouters into a liffeyette."[8] A Dublin river is thus used to evoke an early memory, as the River Boyne would have inspired a tale of Fionn or of St. Patrick. During his *macgnimartha*, HCE "learned to speak from hand to mouth till he could talk earish with his eyes shut,"[9] an obvious retelling of Fionn's assumption of illuminating knowledge by putting his hand (or thumb) into his mouth. As an adult businessman, HCE "catches his check at banck of Indgangd and endurses his doom at chapel exit,"[10] geographical reference to his Chapelizod pub and reaffirmation of HCE/Fionn's banishment to hell in the eyes of the Christian elders.

The magnanimity of Fionn MacCumhaill and Joyce's awareness of the reduction of the hero also relate to the *Acallamh*. As "escape-master-in-chief from all sorts of houding places,"[11] HCE is Fionn released from *bruidhean* entrapments and an eel-like HCE who escapes punishment. As "first of the fenians, roi des fainéants" (king of the sloths), HCE/Fionn has diminished in stature with the passing of time and the introduction of a new heroic figure, Jesus Christ. Because HCE/Fionn has been slandered, he must be considered timeless, one who moves in "vicous cicles yet remews the same"[12] (a Viconian clue in a punning figure of speech) in order to avoid the closure final judgment would impose on him.

HCE/Fionn's immunity from death actually fosters the debate over the disposition of Fionn's soul in Ossianic tradition. HCE "hands his secession to the new patricius but plumps plebmatically for the bloody old centuries,"[13] a reminder of the glories of Fionn's past and of the establishment of a new order. Fionn's stoical defiance of final judgment is expressed when he "went within a sheet of tissue paper of the option of three goal"[14] (which I see as heaven, hell, or purgatory for a Fenian). HCE/Fionn is "excruciated," which Joyce may have blended from "excommunicated" and "crucified," for both punishments have been dealt to Fionn MacCumhaill in Irish folklore.

Because the *Acallamh na Senorach* contains tales of paganism and Christianity, it represents a struggle between the Old Dispensation and the New, one that is reflected in the father/son struggle of many Irish literary works. Joyce had already handled some aspects of filial resistance in *Ulysses*, ranging from Stephen Dedalus' anger at the usurpation of his country by the Roman Catholic Church and England, to his personal conflict with Simon Dedalus and his final merging of identity with Leopold Bloom. In *Finnegans Wake*, Joyce repeats the motif with another rebellious son, who is represented by twins, an idea that had germinated in *Ulysses*, in the Hamnet/Rudy Bloom connection of the novel. HCE/Fionn is metamorphosed into the Russian General of Book Two, Chapter Three of *Finnegans Wake*, who is shot by Buckley, but the incident is foreshadowed in the riddle of Book One, Chapter Six, with "beschotten by a buckeley." John Kelleher postulates that Buckley derives from the Irish *buachaill* or boy,[15] so the ritual murder of the father may be reenacted. But the use of "beschotten" may also derive from "begotten," so that Stephen Dedalus' idea of being one's own father may apply to *Finnegans Wake*. The two vaudeville comedians of this novel, Butt and Taff (Shem and Shaun), gradually merge into the identity of Buckley ("now one and the same person") and shoot the foreign general, whose identity they eventually assume. The patricide/slaying of the Russian General, defiler of Irish sod, is Ossianic through Shem's identification with Ossian in his response to the second of the twelve riddles in Book One, Chapter Six ("make the Rageous Ossean kneel and quaff a lyre!"),[16] in his acquiescence to and fusion with Shaun in Book Two, Chapter Two, and in "their" murder of a foreigner or usurper, for St. Patrick was not Irish. The authority figure "falls by Goll's gillie," as Fionn's father was killed by Goll of the clan Morna and Fionn must fight the son of Morna. In Ossianic tradition, the son alternately defends and destroys the father, until he becomes the father himself.

The pattern repeats in *Finnegans Wake*, as Shaun adopts some of his father's undesirable traits. As the ruthless politician Juan, the false priest, and the sleeping Yawn, he grows into a recumbent Fionn MacCumhaill, who is a manifestation of HCE. Yawn is tried by four judges in Book Three, just as his father was in Book One, and is eventually recognized as one with the father in parody of the trinity: "Three in one, one and three/Shem and Shaun are the shame that sunders em./Wisdom's son, folly's brother."[17]

Although the focus of the *Acallamh na Senorach* is not on the role of women in Fenian legend, but rather on the argument between Oisin and St. Patrick, there are still portions of the folktale recordings that refer to Diarmaid and Grainne. Joyce, via metmorphosis of his characters in *Finnegans Wake*, reintroduces Diarmaid, friend of Fionn and Oisin, who unwittingly becomes the cause of Fionn's bride's betrayal. While the elopement of Diarmaid and Grainne is sometimes attributed to her having put a *geis* on the young warrior, and other times explained as the result of the female's victimization by enchantment (in the fashion of the *Tristan and Isolde* legend), Joyce handles the tale as one that exemplifies the sorrow caused by feminine interference. A crude reference to the Grainne legend surfaces in the first riddle of Book One, Chapter Six: "made up to Miss MacCormack ni Lacarthy who made off with Darly Dermod, swank and swarthy; once diamond cut garnet new dammat cuts groany."[18] And Shem and Shaun are probably the figure metamorphosed into Fionn's betrayer, Diarmaid, for shortly after this allusion, HCE/Fionn is "buckshot back shattered," thus tricked and murdered by his sons (though Fionn is simply a cuckold, he is metaphorically shot in the back). The contemporary source for Grainne is most likely Issy, the daughter of HCE and his wife, Anna Livia Plurabelle, especially as the young girl sometimes merges with the identity of her mother, HCE/Fionn's wife. Issy, whose name hails from the Celtic legend of *Tristan and Isolde*, source tale for Diarmaid and Grainne, also figures in a story that combines cuckoldry and incest, in Book Two, Chapter Four of *Finnegans Wake*. Tristram (Shem/Shaun) vies with King Mark (HCE) over Yseult (Issy): "when he was kiddling and cuddling and bunnyhugging scrumptious his colleen bawn and dinkum belle, an oscar sister."[19] This colleen bawn or girl woman elicits the incestuous attentions of the father and brother(s). In choosing the King Mark analogy, Joyce repeats the Fionn/Diarmaid/Grainne triangle, with the added complication of the Oscar sister, who would be a granddaughter of King Mark or Fionn. The metamorphoses protect the characters, structurally, from recognition of their incestuous thoughts and deeds, although such acts would not comprise *geis* violation in Ossianic tradition.

If women of the *Acallamh* are portrayed as tricksters or deceivers, in the recitations of Caoilte or Oisin, their wiles are not limited to those of Grainne. In Book Two, Chapter Three, Joyce begins a passage that alludes to Fionn's betrayal and moves on to the entrapment of Oisin: "fummuccumul with a graneen aveiled. Playing down the slavery touch. Much as she was when the fancy cutter out collecting milestones espied her aseesaw on a fern. So nimb, he said dat a dew. Between Furr-y-Ben and Ferr-y-Bree. In this tear Vikloe vich he lofed. The smiling ever."[20] Nimb, a form of Niamh, seduced Fionn's son Oisin and led him away to Fairyland, Tir na nOg. The threat posed by women in traditional Gaelic writings endures in the *Acallamh* and in the metamorphosed females of *Finnegans Wake*.

Yet this "rule" does not always apply to ALP. As the Virgin Mary, Mother of Christ, Anna Livia Plurabelle would best fit in the Christian tales offered by St. Patrick in the *Acallamh*, scarcely assuming the role of temptress. But HCE is a publican and as such is sometimes associated with St. Patrick, who, by legend, brought whiskey to the Irish. As the wife of the "unnamed nonirishblooder that becomes a Greenislender overnight,"[21] ALP would have to abandon her virginal role, and she is, appropriately, a "Bringer of Plurabilities," a link between the pagan and Christian tales. As a Celtic heroine, she protects her maligned spouse in her "mamafesta" or manifesto, paying tribute to the many dimensions of HCE and vouchsafing his concealed identity. As Belinda the hen, ALP scratches out the Letter, which appears, as Patrick McCarthy notes, in every chapter of *Finnegans Wake*, dismembered like Osiris and Earwicker himself.[22] As Lilith and India, ALP shares in the responsibility for the crime; and as Eve, she assumes guilt for bringing sin into the world.

But ALP's metamorphoses best situate her in Ossianic legend when she assumes forms that relate to geographical places, evoking the *dinnsenchas* lore of high, holy places. Her alleged profligate begavior is obscured through river name changes, and her shape-changing into elements of nature—a cloud or the waters of the River Liffey—gives her an enduring quality and transient properties at the same time. She is protected from spatial and chronological strictures, thus she goes on forever. Though Brendan O'Hehir takes pains to prove that the origin of ALP's name is less likely to be found in Abha na Life than in the root *eanach*, meaning marsh or fen (and yielding "Fenegans Wick"),[23] it is still significant that her name is connected with a fluid source. It is also true that Fenian lore is associated with the River Boyne, as mentioned earlier, and not the Liffey, as earliest Irish settlements were not coastal but inland . But then Dublin, too, would not be a center for Fenian tales, so Joyce's geographical allusions are imitative in structure and well suited to the device of metamorphosis. ALP is thus allied with the River Lee through "The Shandon Bells"; and the washerwomen of Book One, Chapter Six include the names of many Irish rivers in a huge catalogue of rivers of the world, as they gossip about ALP. Their evocation of river names and river movement reminds us of the fascination with geography in medieval recordings of Irish folktales and of the elusiveness granted by the change of shape: "Rinse them out and aston along with you! Where did I stop? Never stop! Continuarration! You're not there yet. I amstel waiting. Garonne, garonne!"[24] Their final metamorphosis into tree and stone or stem and stone again connects with Fenian lore, for Irish stone monuments are often called beds of Diarmaid and Grainne.[25]

By adopting new forms in virtually every chapter of *Finnegans Wake*, Joyce's characters could enact their conflicts while maintaining a distance from their true selves. Even the depraved sexual desires of HCE as Honuphrius, ALP as Anita, and their children, Shem, Shaun, and Issy as Jeremias, Eugenius, and Felicia are expressed in the context of names that belong to a distant, pagan past.

But the most redemptive metamorphosis in *Finnegans Wake* is that which ALP undergoes, when she closes the myth with her final monologue. As Fionn's widow, Kate of Ireland, she reshapes herself into the river of Dublin. Clive Hart comments that the giant Fionn and the Liffey (HCE and ALP) lie in the attitude of Bloom and Molly of *Ulysses*, mutually opposed in bed.[26] ALP's last metamorphosis provides a female endnote to the myth. She thereby connects *Finnegans Wake* with the epic *Tain* and Joyce's earlier work, *Ulysses*, with Tantric philosophy and with forgiveness. But she also reminds us that the themes of the *Acallamh* have pervaded the novel: "Ourselves, oursouls alone. At the site of salvocean."[27] The Sinn Fein reference, in its appeal for solidarity, reechoes the Ossianic legends ("save Oisin") in its goal to preserve Irish folklore.

GEIS VIOLATION IN *FINNEGANS WAKE*: INDICTMENT IN A BALLAD

In the tradition of Celtic mythological and folklore recordings, each hero is provided with a *geis* or *geasa*, the number of these increasing with the hero's status. While the interdictions may not coincide with actions that are viewed as sinful in the Christian tradition, the violation of pagan interdiction and the commission of sin are related in that both bring about severe consequences ranging from guilt or loss of honor to death and dismemberment. Fionn MacCumhaill, like Bloom of *Ulysses*, pays the price of domestication through his involvement with women; Cuchulainn is mortally wounded when he consumes dog flesh; Stephen Dedalus agonizes over his refusal to honor a mother's request.

In *Finnegans Wake*, punishment of the hero for geis breaking rings throughout the work. It is less important to determine excatly what the tavernkeeper did in Phoenix Park than it is to note that his trial and suffering are unending, and, like

Fionn in the *Acallamh*, he must be defended in absentia. HCE
has evidently eaten of the metaphorical Tree of Knowledge and
must now pay a price: "he touched upon this tree of livings in
the middenst of the garereden."[28] Joyce parodies the notion of
joy over the fall of man, with "O Phoenix Culprit," a pun on
"o felix culpa," and its cause of a promise of redemption: "O
felicitous culpability, sweet bad cess to you for an archetype."[29]
Like the commission of original sin, Celtic *geis* violation is always recognized in the context of the tale, and the effect it
produces is permanent. Because HCE's sin is so great, no accu-
sation can be too base: "Ever read of that greatgrandlandfather
of our visionbuilders. Baaboo, the bourgeoismeister, who
thought to touch both himmels at the punt of his risen stiff-
staff and how wishywashy sank the waters of his thought?"[30]

Joyce implies that HCE/Fionn seeks some forbidden
knowledge (*imbas forosna?*) and, like fallen Adam, may not
achieve redemption but must die and wait for a savior and baptism. The boundary that HCE has overstepped appears to be
one of a sexual nature, whether it is voyeurism, incest, homo-
sexuality, infidelity, exhibitionism, or all of these. He is
charged with the crime(s) in "The Ballad of Persse O'Reilly,"
introduced in Book One, Chapter Two, a ballad of which we
hear the refrain many times. And Joyce's invention of a folk
ballad to indict HCE reestablishes the significance of traditional Irish oral and written sources, among other purposes.

An examination of some occurrences of the ballad reveals
how the sin or *geis* breaking of the father engenders patricide
and connects to the *Hamlet* motif of *Ulysses*. To begin with,
HCE/Fionn/Humpty Dumpty is felled by the "butt" of the
Magazine Wall, an allusion to Buckley's (Butt/Taff's) shooting
of the Russian General/HCE/Fionn. HCE also appears in the
song as "He'll Cheat E'erawan," which may encompass both
hell and Samuel Butler's *Erewhon*, or utopic heaven. He is also
the owner of the bucket shopstore (a Buckley clue), but he is
"Down Bargainweg, Lower," which implies that HCE/Fionn

has not gained entrance to heaven, as suggested in the *Acallamh*.

But the ballad is first sung in the shadow of Parnell's monument, as Adaline Glasheen points out,[31] which joins HCE with a man whose career has been ruined by a woman, and whose actual physical death was blamed on her, in *Ulysses*. Further, the title of the ballad, which names the offender Persse O'Reilly, suggests death by poisoning through the ear ("percer oreille"), bringing the song back to *Hamlet/Ulysses*. As King Hamlet was supposedly poisoned through the ear by Claudius, Bloom reflects on this in conjunction with the musings on his own father's self-poisoning ("and in the porches of mine ear did pour"). HCE's compulsion to know that which he should not adds substance to Brendan O'Hehir's argument that his name, Humphrey, derives from the same source as the name *Hamlet*.[32]

The ballad repeats a theme of *Hamlet*, Fenian folktales, and other Irish folklore in that it reiterates the warning of the danger inherent in the female. King Hamlet, Fionn, and HCE all fail to heed this *geis*, for "our heavyweight heathen Humphrey (all three)/Made bold a maid to woo."[33] And, of course, the Persse/*percer* association frequently implies loss of virginity in *Finnegans Wake*. But it also indicates incest, for as Honuphrious, HCE/O'Reilly is considered to have committed this sin, involving the "droit d'oreiller" with Felicia, an unnatural act expressed through a pun on his name, the French for "pillow," and a Celtic pagan ritual reserving the first night with a virgin for the king.

The ballad is distinctly pagan and Ossianic when HCE is called "Fingal MacOscar Onesine," a distorted genealogy of Fionn, his son Oisin, and his grandson Oscar. And he is treated as the Fionn of the *Dialogues with St. Patrick* when "the whole audience perseguired and pursuited him olla podrida) outbroke much yellachters from owners in the heall,"[34] a persecuted fallen pagan in hell with his *fennidi*. As St. Pursey

Orelli, who "gave Luiz-Marios Josephs their loyal devouces to be offered up missas for vowts widders,"[35] HCE/Fionn is Christianized; but his soul is damned to eternal punishment when he is "keenhearted by the circuminsistence of the Parkes O'Rarelys,"[36] thus *caoined* or mourned by his progeny, who pled in his behalf.

Joyce even uses the ballad with autobiographical overtones, as he argues for pagan values, in the manner of Caoilte and Oisin: "What do you mean by Jno Citizen and how do you think of Jas Pagan? Compost liffe in Difblin by Pierce Egan with the baugh in Baughkley of Fino Ralli."[37] James, the pagan son, supplants the father, John, as Buckley (Shem/Shaun/ Oisin) holds the bow or gun or phallus that pierces or finished O'Reilly (HCE/Fionn). But "ralli" may also rally, as King Hamlet's ghost resurfaces to tend to unfinished business, and HCE/Fionn is resurrected in the preservation of folklore effected by the *Colloquy with the Elders*. "O'rally, O rally, O rally! Phlenxty, O rally! To what lifelike thyne of the bird can be. See you somany matters. Haze sea east to osseania."[38] The reference to Oisin is no longer disguised, for HCE/Fionn/O'Reilly must become "balladproof" (bullet-proof) and "unperceable" and as strong as the Irish patriot, Padraic Pearse. Although Fionn MacCumhaill has "sinned" in the eyes of the Christian saint in that he was unaware of, thus unable to accept, Christ, he endures a fortunate fall. This fall, celebrated in the ballad, prompts the debate of Oisin and St. Patrick, which inspires the recording of the legends of Fionn MacCumhaill.

REWORKING MYTH: CHRONICLES AND LETTER WRITERS

In the mythic novel *Ulysses*, Joyce reworks a history of Molly Bloom in such a way that the reader is ultimately confused about what actually did take place. Joyce infuses the novel with allusions to ancient Irish mythology, and he provides a deliberately clouded secular history of Bloom, thereby managing to prevent his take from becoming static or fixed. Because it blends what might have been with what was, Molly's final monologue affirms that we have been in the realm of myth.

Irish mythology and Irish folktales are logical sources for such a narrative technique because they, too, encompass multiple versions of popular tales. From the Ulidian Cycle to the Fenian Cycle, basic themes are reworked and repeated, generating slightly different versions each time. Margot Norris argues that the repetition of actions in *Finnegans Wake* is more compulsive and irrational than logical.[39] But an essay by Mary Helen Thuente probably best explains how, in *Finnegans Wake*, Joyce fashions myth in a way that only appears to defy logic. In transferring the oral tradition of the Gaelic storyteller to the written page, Joyce demonstrates how storytelling is a dynamic process that synthesizes mythic tales of the remote past with legends and folktales of more recent history.[40] Such a synthesis calls for a continual retelling and makes it an exercise in frustration to delineate among Joyce's variations on the themes of *Finnegans Wake*.

The "compulsion" to recreate the incriminating Letter of this novel, to retry HCE, to repeat the history of Ireland, and to reconstruct fables stems from a necessity to keep myth alive through constant change. As modern folklorist Ruth Sawyer explains: "There is a kind of death to every story when it leaves the speaker and becomes impaled for all time on clay tablets or the written and printed page."[41] Joyce's solution to this problem was to write no definitive final version of the myth of HCE, so that the tale could stay alive in the reader's mind. He also avoids closure by allowing the story to be told from the perspectives of several characters. While this strategy is not unique to Joyce (certainly Faulkner explores multiple perspectives in *The Sound and the Fury*), there is an inimitable fusion of multiple accounts of an incident that mirror chronicles of pagan and Christian Irish history that span centuries.

HCE/Fionn, a pre-Christian and Catholic hero, cannot die until his story has been told and retold, during which process his death becomes unbelievable. Joyce warns us of the transformations that will result from repetition: "Now let the centuple celves of my egourge as Micholas de Cusack calls them—all of whose I in my hereinafter of course by recourse demission me—by the coincidance of their contraries reamalgamerge in that indentity of undiscernibles."[42]

Earwicker is accused of a multidimensional undisclosed crime of a sexual nature, expressed, in metaphor, as knocking at the door of his own home or "according to his own story, he was a process server and was merely trying to open zozimus bottlop stoub by mortially hammering his magnum bonum (the curter the club the sorer the savage) against the bludget gate for the boots about the swan."[43] But his crime was committed so long ago that witnesses and participants are long dead, so the story may be reinvented in many ways. Similarly, if Fionn MacCumhaill were truly based on one of the original *firbolgs* of Ireland, the distancing effect of time would allow for diverse tellings of his adventures. Only certain repeated elements, such as Fionn's battle with Goll MacMorna, or, in *Finnegans Wake*, HCE's battle with his accusers, assure us that the myths have the same origin.

The fixed structure of HCE's myth in *Finnegans Wake* allows Patrick McCarthy to outline the "1-2-3-4 Theory," in which Earwicker is always the sole offender in a deed perpetrated on or instigated by two females, witnessed by three males (generally soldiers), and reported by four old men.[44] HCE is also judged by twelve jurors, customers, or apostles at each trial, and the verdict of guilty is always accompanied by the girl detective just before HCE protests his innocence in Book Three: "Have you ever weflected, wepowtew, that the evil what though it was willed might nevewtheless lead somehow on to good towards the genewality?"[45]

The charges against HCE are most effectively summed up in the famous Letter, which, like the characters of the novel, undergoes many metamorphoses. Beginning with the fragment scratched from the mud heap by Belinda the hen (ALP) in Book One, Chapter Five, and progressing to the riddles posed by the professor (Book Six), the missive illuminates the many conflicts surounding HCE and his family. More important, the alterations in the Letter call to mind the distorting effect of time and the imposition of personal touch of the writer. Such variables also affected the chronicling of the history of Ireland and of Irish folktales. *The Annals of the Four Masters*, a popular name for the *Annala Rioghachta Eireann*, which Patrick C. Power clarifies was actually composed by six Gaelic literary men, may be a source for the Letter of *Finnegans Wake*. As he explains, Brother Michael, who was known as An Brathair Bocht Michael, or poor Friar Michael, was charged with the task of overseeing a recording of Irish history, between the years 1632 and 1635.[46] In an initial appearance of the Letter (Book One, Chapter Five), a reference to "poor Father Michael" and a source for ALP's name might be found in the Gaelic title of the chronicles (*Annala*). But, more significantly, like the seventeenth-century recordings, the Letter of *Finnegans Wake* mirrors the style of each writer and reflects the information secured by that writer.

Little Kevin/Shaun's witnessing of Belinda's discovery of the first Letter and his discovery of the Ardagh chalice in *Finnegans Wake*, a chalice which, by legend, was actually dug up from underground by a young boy digging for potatoes, connects the Letter to the eighth century. And Shem/Joyce's identification with the sixth-century Irish saint Colmcille, who had surreptitiously copied a gospel or psalter that belonged to St. Fingan[47] (for Shem is accused of forging the Letter, and Joyce undoubtedly borrows ideas from universal literary sources), also bears out the association of the Letter with the *Book of*

Kells, for the manuscript emanated from monasteries that Colmcille had founded. The introduction of the sigla establishes a relationship between the Letter and the illuminated eighth-century manuscript, with all of its decorations and embellishments. Its missing signature in Book One, Chapter Five may recall Queen Victoria's historic visit to Trinity College to view the manuscript, when she mistakenly thought that the anonymous monastic works (composed, primarily, of a recording of the four gospels of the New Testament) required her signature.[48] Joyce hints at this with "it was a habit not to sign letters always."[49] Finally, the *Book of Kells* may have been composed in Iona, the Hebridean island, away from Ireland, out of fear of Viking invasions and possible destruction of the manuscript, just as *Finnegans Wake* was composed abroad by an exile.

But regardless of its inspiration, the Letter of *Finnegans Wake* must, like the gospels of Matthew, Mark, Luke, and John, undergo stylistic changes, though admittedly to a much greater degree. When it appears in the long riddle of Chapter One, Book Six, it recounts Ossianic legends (as discussed in the section on metamorphosis); when it resurfaces in Book Two, Chapter Two, in the form of a night letter composed by three children to their parents, it speaks of a sin committed by ancestors of another, distant age: "With our best youlldied greedings to Pep and Memmy and the old folkers below and beyant."[50] In Book Three, Chapter Three, the Letter is constructed as a sermon, Shaun/Juan's Lenten appeal for chastity, an epistle from a false priest to twenty-eight February daughters and his sister Issy. He praises Issy's "old world tales of homespinning and derringdo and dieobscure and daddyho,"[51] calling for diaspora; and he recalls traditional monastic chroniclings with "Columbian nights" (St. Columba or St. Columbanus, sixth/seventh-century founders of monasteries), and with "Brendan's mantle whitening the Kerribrasilian sea."[52] But while Shaun's allusions associate the Letter with Viking inva-

sions and Irish and other saints, they do not disguise the theme
of the Letter, which is the *geis* violation or sin of HCE and
family. Issy's reply to Juan in Book Three, Chapter Two, with
a biblical Veronican handkerchief turned into a love letter (for
Shem), reassures Juan that "you can trust me that though I
change thy name though not the letter."[53] Since Shem and
Shaun are one, Issy's incestuous offer can truly be with the
same letter, for Shaun/Juan, the priest, desires that Issy (and
other women) remain chaste for his pleasure. And if the twin
sons are but new incarnations of the father, as Issy is sometimes her mother, the sin is shared by all of the Earwickers.

Joyce reworks the theme of the Letter in ALP's accusatory
missive of Book Three, Chapter Three, which takes on a different tone from her original manifesto of Book One, Chapter
Five. As both HCE's wife and the temptress in Phoenix Park,
she submits a version of the incident that attests to the man's
guilt and to her own: "I will confess to his sins and blush me
further."[54] But the sin is applicable to all mankind, as the *Book
of Kells* contains universal lessons. And the *Annals of the Four
Masters* recount the history of the Gaelic race, as the letters of
Finnegans Wake tell of Fionn, Oisin, Viking invasions of Ireland, and St. Patrick. Therefore, the final draft of the Letter, in
Book Four, composed by ALP, derives from both sources. It
offers a defense of husband and family in general, along with
Irish folklore: "Mucksrats which bring up uhrweckers they
will come to know good."[55] Here she indicts the hour-wakers
or alarm clocks, who would stir up trouble, while at the same
time acknowledges the positive effect of reviving Earwicker or
a sleeping Fionn and his history. She also asserts that her husband will be pardoned his sins, as the Fenian warrior will be
granted salvation: "So may the low forget him their trespasses
against Molloyd O'Reilly, that hugglebeddy fann, now about
to get up, the hartiest that Coolock ever!"[56] HCE/Fionn, an
innocent, must be resuscitated and kept alive, like traditional
Irish writings. But only repetition, even with the changes and

inaccuracies that result from the passing of time and the genera-
tion of new myth, can guarantee its preservation.

NOTES

1. James MacKillop, *Fionn MacCumhaill: Celtic Myth in English Literature* (Syracuse: Syracuse University Press, 1986) p. 181.

2. Patrick C. Power, *A Literary History of Ireland* (Cork: Mercier Press, 1969), pp. 39-40.

3. MacKillop, *Fionn MacCumhaill: Celtic Myth in English Literature*, p. 179.

4. James Joyce, *Finnegans Wake* (1939; rpt. New York: Viking, 1967), p. 126.

5. Adaline Glasheen, *Third Census of Finnegans Wake* (Berkeley: University of California Press, 1977), p. lxxii.

6. *Finnegans Wake*, p. 125.

7. Ibid., p. 134.

8. Ibid., p. 126.

9. Ibid., p. 130.

10. Ibid., p. 127.

11. Ibid., p. 127.

12. Ibid., p. 134.

13. Ibid., p. 129.

14. Ibid., p. 139.

15. John Kelleher, "Identifying the Irish Printed Sources for *Finnegans Wake*," *Irish University Review* 1, no. 2 (1971), p. 172.

16. *Finnegans Wake*, p. 139.

17. Ibid., p. 526.

18. Ibid., p. 137.

19. Ibid., p. 384.

20. Ibid., p. 375.

21. Ibid., p. 378.

22. Patrick McCarthy, "The Structures and Meanings of *Finnegans Wake*," in *A Companion to Joyce Studies*, ed. Zack Bowen and James Carens (Westport, Conn.: Greenwood Press, 1984), p. 577.

23. Brendan O'Hehir, *A Gaelic Lexicon for Finnegans Wake and a Glossary for Joyce's Other Works* (Berkeley: University of California Press, 1967), pp. 355-356.

24. *Finnegans Wake*, p. 205.

25. Michael Begnal and Grace Eckley, *Narrator and Character in Finnegans Wake* (Lewisburg, Pa.: Bucknell University Press, 1975), p. 192.

26. Clive Hart, *Structure and Motif in Finnegans Wake* (Evanston, Ill.: Northwestern University Press, 1962), p. 205.

27. *Finnegans Wake*, p. 623.

28. Ibid., p. 350.

29. Ibid., p. 263.

30. Ibid., pp. 191-192.

31. Glasheen, *Third Census of Finnegans Wake*, p. xxxii.

32. O'Hehir, *A Gaelic Lexicon for Finnegans Wake and a Glossary for Joyce's Other Works*, p. 387.

33. *Finnegans Wake*, p. 46.

34. Ibid., p. 92.

35. Ibid., p. 243.

36. Ibid., p. 354.

37. Ibid., p. 447.

38. Ibid., p. 593.

39. Margot Norris, *The Decentered Universe of Finnegans Wake* (Baltimore: Johns Hopkins University Press, 1974), p. 25.

40. Mary Helen Thuente, "'Traditional Innovations': Yeats and Joyce and the Irish Oral Tradition," *Mosaic* 12, no. 3 (1979), p. 102.

41. Ruth Sawyer, *The Way of the Storyteller* (Middlesex, Eng.: Penguin 1942), p. 59.

42. *Finnegans Wake*, pp. 49-50.

43. Ibid., p. 63.

44. McCarthy, "The Structures and Meanings of *Finnegans Wake*," p. 571.

45. *Finnegans Wake*, p. 523.

46. Powers, *A Literary History of Ireland* (Cork: The Mercier Press, 1969), p. 79.

47. O'Hehir, *A Gaelic Lexicon for Finnegans Wake*, p. 376.

48. Frank Delaney, *The Celts* (Boston: Little, Brown, and Co., 1986), p. 134.

49. *Finnegans Wake*, pp. 114-115.

50. Ibid., p. 308.

51. Ibid., p. 431.

52. Ibid., p. 444.

53. Ibid., p. 459.
54. Ibid., p. 494.
55. Ibid., p. 615.
56. Ibid., pp. 615-616.

CHAPTER 4

Flann O'Brien:
At Swim-Two-Birds, *The Third Policeman*—Temporal and Spatial Incongruities

The epic novels of James Joyce, *Ulysses* and *Finnegans Wake*, are literally works that contain realistic and fantastic elements, some of which may be found in Irish myth, legend, and folklore. Although Joyce's writing may be examined via Freudian psychoanalytic approach or Viconian philosophical application, it is rooted in the tradition of Irish folklore. Therefore, we may draw parallels between some of the modern devices Joyce uses and those that stem from Gaelic sources, such as metamorphosis and *geis* violation.

In the literature of Flann O'Brien, however, the situation often appears to be reversed, in that the fantastic elements from Irish tradition overpower the modern plot devices. Although *At Swim-Two-Birds* and *The Third Policeman* are both modern novels, composed respectively in 1939 and 1940, they are close to Celtic myth in their timelessness and free blending of fantasy and reality. They are perhaps best approached as Celtic myths composed in the modern age. When Bernard Benstock comments that O'Brien has a problem bridging the distance between myth and reality,[1] he does not allow for the complete authorial control that O'Brien has inherited from the *seanachie* or from the experimental nature of his writing style. Unlike the novelist who adheres to linear plot development or who allows for some degree of predictability, O'Brien relies on the surprise effects of illogical sequences of events, impossible character combinations, and anachronisms to engage his reader's interest. And, where Joyce confines such anomalies to chapters or episodes that occur in a nonwaking state, O'Brien gives free rein to fantasies within reality in the state of full consciousness in the first novel and in presumed consciousness in the second. Like the traditional storyteller, O'Brien is able to create characters who conduct social intercourse with characters from myth and legend. When he projects his fantasy into the world of the nonliving, as in the inferno of *The Third Policeman*, O'Brien traverses the boundaries of time and space, and mythological possibilities increase.

In a letter of October 3, 1938, to his editor of *At Swim-Two-Birds*, Mr. Heath, O'Brien noted the change of a character, "Angel," from "good spirit" to "Good Fairy" because: "fairy corresponds more closely to 'Pooka,' removes any suggestion of the mock religious and establishes the thing on a mythological plane."[2] But the elements that link *At Swim-Two-Birds* with the world of Irish myth extend beyond the obvious, such as the inclusion of a character named Finn MacCool, the tale of mad Sweeny, or the presence of the pooka. It is O'Brien's use of devices that defy time and space in his two earliest novels that unites them structurally and thematically with Irish myth. His creation of the concepts he calls aestho-autogamy, molecule exchange, and omnium, while satirizing theories of physics, also corresponds to the notion of peculiarities found in Irish heroes and the mystical elements of Catholicism.

As Richard F. Peterson rightly observes, the idea of the writer's ability to create living characters who are fully grown at birth, or aestho-autogamy (in *At Swim-Two-Birds*) is related to a character's power of manipulating time and space, or of omnium (in *The Third Policeman*), for these processes change reality.[3] Robert Alter views the distortions of reality in the author's first novel as an attempt to create a self-reflexive work, as he explains in *Partial Magic*, but we must remember that myth involves continual retelling of a tale, during which process the "facts" change shape. The self-consciousness of the writer is as focused on elucidating the reader about mythmaking as it is on pondering the fate of the novel as form. Reworkings of plot resemble metahistorical tendencies, as ideas are continually reedited; and, in their inclusion of materials and facts from many genres and ages, they defy the basic principles of physics. Thus O'Brien's parodic treatment of the average individual's ability to grasp the theory of relativity, in *The Third Policeman*, is concurrent with temporal and spatial incongruities in Irish mythology. The legendary dispute of Oisin with St. Patrick, after he emerges from a Rip van Winkle-like sleep of three hundred years, synthesizes temporal and atemporal worlds, for historical Ireland had undergone conversion to Christianity by the fifth century and the pagan hero is just a very old man. Preternatural abilities and experiences, abundant in source works, form a bond between O'Brien's early novels and Irish source works.

Because *At Swim-Two-Birds* and *The Third Policeman* feature so many characteristics from Irish traditional writings, I draw attention to those that demonstrate the unreliability of time and space and how this instability allows traditional elements to function. Chronology is often deliberately obscured in Celtic myth, numbers being symbolic rather than accurate, in many instances. Cuchulainn's birth as a son of three years reiterates the importance of the number three in Celtic mythology more than it attempts to keep time. O'Brien's apparent obsession with triads in *At Swim-Two-Birds* therefore has nothing to do with chronology or ordinal events. The character Orlick Trellis' novel has three beginnings, and O'Brien's exterior novel ends with the German who was fond of the number three: "He went home one evening and drank three cups of tea with three lumps of sugar in each cup, cut his jugular with a razor three times and scrawled with a dying hand on a picture of his wife good-bye, good-bye, good-bye."[4]

This number coincides with the mystical Christian symbol of the Trinity, foreshadows the title of O'Brien's next book, and, through the use of three renditions of a tale, reminds us of the multiple tellings of any story or myth. Sublimating or obscuring the role of chronology, O'Brien plunges the reader into an atemporal domain, suggesting that a novel may have many different beginnings, all of which may occur at different times, and, in the same vein, that there may be overlaps between the beginnings, as traditional folktales often contain overlapping events from different historical periods. The appearance of Finn MacCool as the creator of fiction, heroic figure from mythology, and modern-day seedy boarding house character provides us with a double vision of the legendary tribal warrior, as Patricia O'Hara points out.[5] It also permits the dissolution of normal chronology and probably upsets many a reader's faith in O'Brien's ability to create either pure fantasy or modern fiction. Unlike *Finnegans Wake*, in which ongoing metamorphoses and restructurings of basic plot are presumed to occur in an unconscious state, much of O'Brien's first novel contains actions that apparently happen in the realm of temporal reality.

By creating an elastic sense of time, O'Brien establishes that all characters of myth, whether of oral tradition or the modern novel, are on the same plane. Literary authors may combine their newly created characters with figures from legend and folklore, engaging in conversation and action with gods, saints, and heroes. As Anne Clissman observes, the pooka and the Good Fairy may travel through a forest inhabited by fictional creatures, and the poet, Jem Casey, may meet the legendary King Sweeny.[6] The narrator in *The Third Policeman* may travel into a zone in which characters may be defined as part horse or part bicycle.

If travel, unhampered by time, allows us to meet fantastic characters in the works of O'Brien, it also underscores his de-

sire to remain close to Irish tradition. As a student of Irish language and literature, who wrote his masters thesis on "Nature
in Irish Poetry,"[7] O'Brien was familiar with tales of the *sid*,
imram or sea voyage adventures, and *bruidhean* tales, all of
which involve suspensions of normal spatial and temporal experience. And the historic accuracy of later renditions of many
traditional legends, which, for example, portray Cuchulainn of
the Ulster Cycle as a Christ figure or Fionn with five wounds
at death, obviously calls for the stretching of spatial and temporal possibilities. But the novel may also operate in logically
contradictory modes of time and space, permitting the inclusion of temporally displaced characters. Clissman notes, too,
that the Battle of Ringsend in *At Swim-Two-Birds* recreates the
cattle raid of the *Tain*.[8] And O'Brien very likely includes cowboys from a movie set in a scene that mimics the epic battle of
Celtic mythology to demonstrate the needlessness of sequential
plot development. He juxtaposes American western, Gaelic
pagan, and Christian heroes: "God, says I, he's doing the Brian
Boru in his bloody tent. (What, at the prayers?)"[9] If the traditional *seanachie* may compress three hundred years into what
seems like a day, then the modern author may create a character who feels that twenty years are but three days. Time, in *At
Swim-Two-Birds*, as we know it, is not subject to any regula-
tors.

O'Brien appears to pursue the agelessness of Ossianic legend
(one that breaks down when the hero touches the earth again)
in his second novel, *The Third Policeman*. When Oisin was removed from the physical world, to the Land of the Young, he
received immunity from the effects of earthly time and the aging process. The narrator of *The Third Policeman* is likewise
removed to a zone in which time has been frozen; the closed
setting of Mathers' house is compared by Joseph Voelker to
the atemporal caves of Celtic lore, milieus in which time does
not pass.[10] Like the confinement of Oisin, the containment of
the narrator hero is a prelude to troubled times and a rude

awakening. And, like the caves to which Voelker alludes, the scene of entrapment serves a magical purpose and subjects the hero to a trial of sorts in an otherworldly trap.

For want of a *ceadach*, or helper figure, the narrator of *The Third Policeman* takes comfort from the voice of his own "soul" (a Christian concept), who is a character named Joe. This entity, intruding in an otherwise pagan setting, enjoys a separate and independent existence at times, and he ultimately separates from the narrator's body. Joe transcends death, politely explaining that he will presumably become part of some atemporal concern: "I do not know, or do not remember, what happens to the like of me in these circumstances. Sometimes, I think that perhaps I might become part of . . . the world, if you understand me."[11]

O'Brien's attempt to portray characters who experience timeless or anachronistic events is successful because he creates settings that are not governed by traditional concepts of time and space. What appears to be a parody of the Quantum Theory of physics is actually, in addition, an expression of disdain for the confining properties of spatial realities. In traditional Irish writings, such limitations simply do not exist. Creatures known as the *fomoire* and *lochlannaig*, demonic pirates or invaders from across the sea, operate in Fenian legends, as do characters from the Tuatha de Danaan, inhabitants of the *sidhe*, or fairy mounds, allegedly the earliest inhabitants of Ireland before mortals.[12] Spatial possibilities are infinite, as figures from unconnected realms merge in one scenario; temporal impossibilities are negated because the door to the other side is always left open.

Unlike Joyce, who carries Earwicker through many dimensions when he is not fully conscious, O'Brien exposes his heroes to temporal and spatial anomalies while they appear to be in full control of the situation. He designs instruments or forces that conquer time, and we see the effects in characters like Dermot Trellis of *At Swim-Two-Birds*, who creates an entity who is fully grown at birth, five feet eight inches in height, and possessed of a special aptitude for mathematics, John Furriskey. "Aestho-autogamy has long been commonplace," explains Trellis, and it "has been the dream of every practising psycho-eugenist the world over."[13] But it is Officer MacCruiskeen who presents the ultimate defiance of physical restrictions, in *The Third Policeman*, as he endeavors to define omnium, a substance that encompasses cheese, braces, and even God, and can convert light into sound: "Omnium is the essential inherent interior essence which is hidden inside the root of the kernel of everything and it is always the same."[14] If fictional life and real life are identical in *At Swim-Two-Birds*, and omnium is everything in *The Third Policeman*, then there can be no certainty of being dead or alive. But O'Brien is no more an illusionist than the primitive mythmaker, who gives equal weight to prophecy and deed, or the physicist, who explains natural phenomena via the existence of universal elements, like the molecule or the transference of matter.

Some of the characteristics of O'Brien's first two novels that attest to his imitation of structural and thematic motifs from Irish folklore were first observed in *Ulysses* and *Finnegans Wake*. Like Joyce, he employs the device of *geis* violation, but in an imitative manner more than as a punitive measure for his disorderly characters. Finn's account of the madness of Sweeny in *At Swim-Two-Birds* reminds us of the sufferings of Joyce's overreaching Earwicker in *Finnegans Wake*, or perhaps of the disillusioned Dedalus of *Ulysses*, whose name, derived from Ovid's *Metamorphosis*, implies that his attempt to reach goals that are too high will cause his wings to melt as he nears the sun. O'Brien tends to use "climbing" monikers, with Dermot and Orlick Trellis, whose reach exceeds their grasp, in the tradition of the "wicker" man Joyce uses for similar purposes. The inclusion of Sweeny in *At Swim-Two-Birds* not only signifies ascension to new heights but introduces a character from another time warp, like the cowboys' anomalous presence in the novel.

A psychoanalytic examination of the ladder or trellis metaphor yields the sexual connotation, with Dermot Trellis appropriately raping Sheila Lamont, who dies after giving birth to a fully grown adult male. Tormented by his own offspring, Orlick, and his fictional characters (who are, in a sense, also his progeny), Dermot, as a writer, violates many Celtic *geasa* in that he plays God through authorial creation. Trellis thereby mirrors the student narrator of *At Swim-Two-Birds*, who could also be O'Brien himself. The dangers of literary pursuits supply even the writer with an interdiction, who shares in the misfortunes of traditional satirists and secular writers of Irish tradition, who dare to overstep their bounds.[15]

The burden of *geis* is finally placed upon the literary critic or collator of criticism in *The Third Policeman*, a point Desmond MacNamara does not fail to take up in his 1994 *Book of Intrusions*, in which he imitates O'Brien's technique. The narrator is led astray in *The Third Policeman*, not because the murder of Mathers will make him wealthy, but because he wishes to publish the "DeSelby Index." As murder itself rarely constitutes *geis* violation in Celtic folklore, it is appropriate that the actual homicide is of secondary importance in this novel, while the theft of ideas is less forgivable. Significantly, O'Brien promotes the idea that *geis* breaking leads to disorder and unreason, whether the taboo is from mythology or modern morality. Once the interdiction is not observed, heroic status is undermined.

O'Brien further reproduces motifs from traditional writings by granting his characters special gifts or peculiarities (sometimes in the form of defects), which mark or delineate their special standing. While Joyce's pointed but limited use of the thematic motif in *Ulysses* was mainly restricted to blindness, O'Brien celebrates physical uniqueness in a fantastic way. The talents of Officer MacCruiskeen in *The Third Policeman* include possession of an invisible spear. He flourishes the weapon, explaining: "It is so thin that maybe it does not exist at all and you could spend an hour trying to think about it and you could put not thought around it in the end."[16] Cuchulainn of the Ulster Cycle carried the Spear of Bolga, which prepared him for battle with the god Bolga or Oengus Bolg, a serious application of the peculiarity (in this instance, an accoutrement); Joyce alluded to the ashplant/sword in *Ulysses* in a seriocomic vein; but O'Brien implements the motif in a completely farcical manner. The magical properties of the spears in all three examples prevail because their heroes/carriers exist in an environment that is not subject to the laws of ordinary sensory perception.

Peculiarities, in fact, abound in *The Third Policeman*. MacCruiskeen has mastered the creation of chests that are so infinitesimally small as to be invisible, and he also boasts of never having to shave. His colleague, Sergeant Pluck, never gains weight and speaks of a grandfather who was a horse for a year before he died. Finally, Sergeant Craddock is a high-jumper, whose athletic prowess calls to mind Cuchulainn's famed salmon leap. This particular endowment also appears in the leaps of Sweeny and the hag of *At Swim-Two-Birds*. In the 1939 novel, Celtic peculiarity is evidenced in the pooka, who, like Fionn, possesses a magical thumb. And, as mentioned above, the writer demonstrates his unique ability to spawn fully developed characters via aestho-autogamy; the abnormal gestation or obscure background of the traditional Irish hero may provide a source for the sudden birth of the O'Brien character, as created by Dermot Trellis.

Spontaneous creation is permitted by temporal immunity, a condition that also allows that characters may be interchangeable from one book to another. Ruth apRoberts explains de-Selby's reemergence in *The Dalkey Archive* (1964), after an initial introduction in *The Third Policeman* (1940), as proof that he is a very real character, "one who has achieved self-realization, under a democratic authorial administration."[17]

But deSelby's time travel is allowable for reasons beyond benevolent authorship; like heroes of traditional Irish writings,
he transcends cycles (literary publication dates, for O'Brien).
Fionn MacCumhaill is first heard of as Lugh, in the oldest
Mythological Cycle or Cycle of the Invasions; he emerges as a
warrior hero in post-Ulidian Fenian folklore; and he endures
in contemporary folklore as the sleeping giant.

Abandoning temporal strictures also allows O'Brien to
combine pagan and Christian mythology in his fiction, as was
done in Irish traditional writings. Just as Fionn was given five
wounds in death at the Battle of Gabhra, where he fought
Cairbre of the Liffey, high king of Tara,[18] Sweeny from *At
Swim-Two-Birds* "comes back" from O'Brien's own translation
of a medieval romance, Buile Suibhne.[19] O'Brien introduces a
figure who may be traced back to Merlin of pre-Christian legend, allowing for a parody of Christianity in the tradition of
The Vision of MacConglinne, providing for a scenario in which
O'Brien expresses contempt for the modern Irishman, who
does not appreciate Gaelic literature, and expressing a lesson of
anger and contrition. Sweeny, in his tree, has accepted his punishment for the breaking of *geis* or commission of sin:

> God has given me life here,
> very bare, very narrow,
> no woman, no trysting,
> no music or trance-eyed sleep.[20]

Like the *fili* or poet of pagan Celtic lore, a seeker of truth,
Sweeny must recite twelve books of poetry, demonstrating
that he has passed an initiatory ordeal of the pre-Christian
bardic tradition. Yet he also acknowledges penance performed
for sins committed against a Christian god.

Dermot Trellis suffers, too, from unacceptable conduct (the
rape of Lamont), prompted by the irresistible qualities of a
woman, and, like Earwicker of *Finnegans Wake*, must face a
judge and twelve jurors, who are one and the same in *At Swim-*

Two-Birds: J. Furriskey, T. Lamont, P. Shanahan, S. Andrews, S. Willard, Mr. Sweeny, J. Casey, R. Kiersey, M. Tracy, Mr. Lamphall, F. MacCool, and Supt. Clohessy, the twelve "apostles" of O'Brien's first novel. His second work contains tales of crime and punishment, too. The wooden-legged narrator loses memory of his own name and is tried for criminal activity throughout *The Third Policeman*. Having lost his frame of reference, like Earwicker, he is apprised of new "commandments," which he must follow to save his soul. The five new rules have absolutely nothing to do with traditional Christian precepts of morality and display the arbitrary nature of pagan *geis*. They include a warning against answering any questions and a caution to apply the brakes first. Further, the narrator must finally accept that he has been executed for violation of the Christian/civil interdiction against murder. But he is additionally punished with chaos and disharmony for having ignored the Celtic/pagan *geis* against the pursuit of taboo knowledge. He must repeat his journey endlessly through an irrational netherworld: "Hell goes round and round. In shape it is circular and by nature it is interminable, and very nearly unbearable."[21] Like Conan Maol or Conan the Bald of Fenian folklore, a figure who does not escape with Fionn and the *fennedi* from a *bruidhean* adventure, the narrator of *The Third Policeman* is never released. Confronted with the face of the deceased Mathers, he must accept the reality of his own death and punishment and remain in a zone that exists beyond time and space. And, like the teller of the Fenian tale, O'Brien introduces pathetic humor in the account of the character's suffering.

Removing imperatives of time and space finally allows O'Brien to develop the structural device of metamorphosis, one that extends from defense mechanisms in Celtic magical tales and myths to mystical transformation or transubstantiation in the Catholic liturgy. The epistemology of Joyce's use of sexual metamorphosis in both *Ulysses* and *Finnegans Wake* is such that characters are able to protect themselves from knowledge of their own taboo desires or practices through disguise. But when O'Brien provides for partial or complete metamorphosis of a character or object, he suggests how the possibilities of form change are infinite in a timeless and spaceless setting. He fuses the Atomic Theory with Irish mythology, resulting in the establishment of the theory that molecular recombination can produce structural changes in human and objects. Fantasy grants science license to assume such possibilities. Jerry McGuire finds the idea in *The Third Policeman* that humans can become part bicycle, and bicycles part human, a metaphor for the reader who becomes fixed in his text.[22] But O'Brien is preserving a mythological device while offering parodic scientific explanations for these physical incongruities. If the Irish pagan god Angus Og could turn King Congal into a goat through magic, then Sergeant Pluck can speak of a grandfather who became part horse because of a scientific formula. The sergeant also explains how a man may have a lot of bicycle in his veins: "If his number is over fifty you can tell it unmistakably from his walk. He will walk smartly always and never sit down and he will lean against the wall with his elbow out and stay like that all night in the kitchen instead of going to bed."[23]

O'Brien offers many unlikely metamorphoses in *At Swim-Two-Birds* in a conversation among Jem Casey, the Pooka, and the Good Fairy. The Pooka inquires whether Casey's wife ever takes on the physical appearance of a kangaroo; he is then reminded by the Good Fairy that she was said to be a broomstick that morning, after admitting that she could just as well be a lump of a carrot. But their attention quickly shifts to the mad Sweeny, who has lighted in a tree and is taken for a bird, then a marsupial, before he is finally recognized as a man.

Through shape-changing, O'Brien destroys the reader's hopes of ever finding structural consistency among the characters and objects of his first two novels, perhaps suggesting that the novel itself ought to be afforded the same degree of flexibility. Indeed, he finds it necessary for some characters or objects to have no shape at all. "I'm glad I have no body" is a pronouncement from the Good Fairy of *At Swim-Two-Birds*, one that is echoed in *The Third Policeman*, when the narrator acknowledges to Joe, "I know you have no body. Except my own, perhaps."[24] The only body we may rely on is the framework of the novel itself, but the structure of the novel, as a genre, may also melt away with time.

O'Brien's characters may metamorphose and defy the laws of time, space, and gravity; and his plots, like the cycles of Irish mythology, Joyce's *Finnegans Wake*, which ends where it has begun, and the inferno of *The Third Policeman*, may be circular in nature. But it is because Flann O'Brien's novels achieve stasis, then introduce incongruities in time-frozen atmospheres, that a myriad of phenomena can take place.

O'Brien continues to experiment with time distortion, time travel, and the properties of physics in his later novel *The Dalkey Archive* (1964), which contains the character of De-Selby, genius and author of the DeSelby Index and object of adulation by the narrator in *The Third Policeman*. Resurfacing as DeSelby (with an upper case D), he is now an inventor/physicist, who has created a substance that is capable of deoxygenating the world and that he names DMP (also an acronym for Dublin Military Police). As a time traveler, he holds conversations beneath the sea with St. Augustine; as a privileged personage, DeSelby has exclusive knowledge that James Joyce is alive and living in Skerries. He leads the character Mick to Joyce, who is found to be writing Catholic pamphlets and is considering a Jesuit vocation (he denies authorship of *Ulysses*).

O'Brien's displacement of characters, incongruous combinations of literary, fictive, and historical figures, and his anachronisms thus go on. But in all of his writing, O'Brien features motifs from traditional Irish source works, heroes from varying epochs, and allusions to Ireland's Christian conversion.

NOTES

1. Bernard Benstock, "The Three Faces of Brian O'Nolan," in *Alive-Alive O!: Flann O'Brien's At Swim-Two-Birds*, ed. Rüdiger Imhof (Totowa, N. J.: Barnes and Noble, 1985), p. 69.

2. Stephen Jones, ed., *A Flann O'Brien Reader* (New York: Viking, 1978), p. 4.

3. Richard F. Peterson, "Flann O'Brien's Timefoolery," *Irish Renaissance Annual* 3 (1982), p. 42.

4. Flann O'Brien, *At Swim-Two-Birds* (New York: Pantheon, 1939), p. 316.

5. Patricia O'Hara, "Finn MacCool and the Bard's Lament in Flann O'Brien's *At Swim-Two-Birds*," *Journal of Irish Literature* 15, no. 1 (1986), p. 56.

6. Anne Clissman, *Flann O'Brien: A Critical Introduction to His Writings* (New York: Barnes and Noble, 1975), p. 139.

7. Ibid., p. 76.

8. Ibid., p. 136.

9. *At Swim-Two-Birds*, p. 82.

10. Joseph C. Voelker, "'Doublends Jined': The Fiction of Flann O'Brien," *Journal of Irish Literature* 12, no. 1 (1983), p. 92.

11. Flann O'Brien, *The Third Policeman* (1940; rpt. New York: Walker and Co., 1967), pp. 161-162.

12. Joseph Falaky Nagy, *The Wisdom of the Outlaw* (Berkeley: University of California Press, 1985), p. 37.

13. *At Swim-Two-Birds*, p. 55.

14. *The Third Policeman*, p. 110.

15. Clissman, *Flann O'Brien: A Critical Introduction to His Writings*, p. 161.

16. *The Third Policeman*, pp. 68-69.

17. Ruth apRoberts, "*At Swim-Two-Birds* and the Novel as Self-Evident Sham," *Éire/Ireland* 6, no. 2 (1971), p. 91.

18. James MacKillop, *Fionn MacCumhaill: Celtic Myth in English Literature* (Syracuse: Syracuse University Press, 1986), p. 24.

19. Clissman, *Flann O'Brien: A Critical Introduction to His Writings*, p. 129.

20. *At Swim-Two-Birds*, p. 93.

21. *The Third Policeman*, p. 200.

22. Jerry McGuire, "Teasing after Death: Metatextuality in *The Third Policeman*," *Éire/Ireland* 16, no. 2 (1981), p. 114.

23. *The Third Policeman*, p. 117.

24. Ibid., p. 90.

CHAPTER 5

Mervyn Wall and Darrell Figgis: The Fursey Novels and *The Return of the Hero*

Flann O'Brien took the title for his novel of 1939, *At Swim-Two-Birds*, from the village of Snamh-da-en, which is situated along the river Shannon, a few miles south of Clonmacnoise. Mervyn Wall moves upriver a bit and provides the historic setting of the medieval monastic center of Clonmacnoise for his first two novels, *The Unfortunate Fursey* (1946) and *The Return of Fursey* (1948).

Wall chooses to construct what Robert Hogan perceives as a satirical fantasy,[1] in which the fantastic elements do not seem to conflict with the basic historical structure. Indeed, just as we know that the precepts of Catholicism were embraced by and assimilated into Celtic legends, so the unbelievable magic occurrences of the Fursey novels seem to take place quite naturally within the monastery of Clonmacnoise. Wall benefits from the Celt's ability to keep one foot in the world of faery and the other in the domain of Catholic dogma. This phenomenon permits him to compose ecclesiastical satire within a Christian novel, thus maintaining a tradition of Irish narrative sources.

One of the earlier Irish writings that provides a model for satire, the *Acallamh na Senorach*, is now recognized as a treatise that serves two purposes: the legendary argument between Caoilte and St. Patrick and Oisin and the saint not only makes sport of the evangelizing of Ireland but also preserves and records Fenian legends. Thus, while Mervyn Wall claims to have been inspired by continental witchcraft beliefs as evidenced in a seventeenth-century collection of ghost stories, adding that he intended the Fursey novels to constitute a satire of such beliefs, as well as of twentieth-century Irish sexual repression,[2] his novels still succeed in portraying a conflict between the forces of pre-Christian and Christian Ireland.

Wall does not, however, carry on these literary rituals by using a formulaic approach to the development of the hero. Instead, he inverts the qualities and experiences of the traditional hero figure, introducing a new spin on the education of the warrior. We learn more or less by contraries; that is, an Irish hero is what the lay brother Fursey is not (just as Brother Furiosus is the antithesis of the good monk). Moreover, it is through the inversion of the characteristics of the Gaelic hero and by Fursey's misadventures that satire is effected.

To begin with, Fursey, the forty-year-old lay brother, is not a seeker-hero, but, to borrow a term from Propp's *Morphology of the Folktale*, a victim-hero.[3] Unlike Cuchulainn, who goes off to slay the hound of Culann, or Fionn, who embarks on a career of outlawry and battles, Fursey chooses the life of a recluse. We learn that the monk "never answered back, partly because in the excess of his humility he believed himself to be the least of men."[4] In all his mediocrity, Fursey is probably the least likely candidate for heroism, but, unlike Shakespeare's Malvolio, he will have greatness thrust upon him.

The dubious distinction that separates Fursey from the other residents of the monastery is an inability to expel the forces of Satan and his entourage from his cell. Fursey's original peculiarity, a stutter or stammer, which prevents him from driving out the demons with prayer, eventually disappears, to be replaced by a limp. This, in turn, is supplanted by the more impressive qualities of sorcery. But his unsought "greatness" cannot be achieved until he is expelled from the once-secure monastic environment, in which he functioned as a parer of edible roots. And his guide, or *ceadach* figure, upon learning of his dismissal, will be a benevolent Lucifer, introducing yet another inversion of a traditional hero tale. As Hogan accurately concludes, the forces upon which Fursey has always relied for protection, the Church and State, abandon him to the forces of demonic persuasion.[5] Lacking the gift of *imbas forosna*, or secret knowledge, and possessing only his faith (which becomes somewhat shaky), Fursey must come to rely on universal and specific helpers from the side of evil as he begins his unsolicited journey.

Wall indulges artfully in reverse play tactics, distorting historical facts for purposes of satire, as Joyce had done in *Ulysses*. Thus the scholarly King Cormac mac Cullenainn, whom Patrick Power calls the last great literary figure of early Christian Ireland,[6] may be reduced to a five-foot-tall monarch weakened by the temptations of women and chastized by the bishop of Cashel (Cormac historically served as both king and bishop). This rearrangement of historical facts allows Wall to expose a Celtic *geis* or taboo concerning women and the greed of the Christian hierarchy. The bishop may cut down all of his trees so that the birds' singing does not provoke sensual thoughts, and he may later allow the Prince of Darkness to enter a trial setting and operate as Fursey's helper because he brings offerings of gold in the guise of an eastern potentate. Wall may unconsciously reproduce here a traditional Irish satire of the greedy cleric, as evidenced in an eighteenth-century work ascribed to St. Columcille, *Tairngire*, or *The Prophecy*, in which it is said that five wounds are inflicted upon the Gaels by outsiders, but a sixth wound comes from within, from an unrighteous clergy.[7] The selfish behavior of the abbot allows him to cast out the hapless lay brother, who will then be forced to violate the interdictions of Catholicism through no fault of his

own. The traditional Gaelic hero is tricked into *geis* breaking
by external, evil forces; Fursey is handed over to the enemy by
his own protectors.

The most grievous sin that Fursey commits is that of trafficking with the devil, though not in a Faustian manner, as he
did not conjure up Satan in the first place. The offense affords
Mervyn Wall an opportunity to recall pagan Ireland again, in
the tradition of the *Acallamh*, when Cuthbert the sorcerer reminds Fursey that demons are a product of Christianity:
"They are a creation of Christianity, while I am the servant of
a more venerable religion; still, demons are all right in their
own place. I have more liking for them than monks and religious jugglers."[8] As an Irish Christian hero, Fursey has obviously broken ecclesiastical law; as a pre-Christian one, he trespasses against no interdiction in his polite albeit reluctant social
intercourse with Satan. Satan, discomfited by the spiritual environment he invades, employs sophistry to gain Fursey's acceptance, urging him to be "a good Christian." If Fursey would
only accept the figures of darkness, he might partake of even
greater assistance. But he remains torn between pragmatic employment of taboo offerings and aesthetic preservation of
Christian beliefs. He is stuck between two worlds.

Fursey truly acquires his powers through sheer happen-
stance. No druidic prophecy precedes his assumption of sorcerer's abilities, which include riding a broomstick and pulling
a rope to secure food and drink. While these powers and mani-
festations are relatively pedestrian, they do serve to distinguish
the lay brother from ordinary men. And they also suggest that
even a christianized Gael may possess magical powers from a
pagan era. When the Gray Mare, Fursey's short-term bride,
breathes her powers into his throat so that she may expire, the
monk is superstitious enough to believe that he has inherited
them. While this woman, as a witch, may not necessarily derive from Irish folklore, as a "hag" she could find her source in
many Irish folktales, in which women hold supernatural

power. At any rate, Fursey believes in her and in the powers she may pass on to him.

Ironically, the devil himself points out quite early in the first of these two novels that he cannot abide superstition. Father Furiosus, the abbot, and Bishop Flanagan are, unfortunately, superstitious ecclesiastics, ready to torture and torment Fursey, as they would any human ridden with demonic spirits. Wall indicts churchmen in a fashion that could easily derive from *The Vision of MacConglinne*, in which the monks are prepared to crucify the poet after they plunge him into the river Lee, until he is saved by a visionary dream. The monks of the Fursey novels possess equal narrowmindedness; indeed, Fursey is even less guilty than the medieval Anier. The bishop explains church policy: "It is accepted principle in witchcraft proceedings that where doubt exists, one should convict. The Church's view is happily summed up in the well-known phrase: 'Burn all; God will distinguish His own.'"[9]

Fursey thereby entrusts his welfare to sorcerers, elementals, and devils. He is granted the services of Albert, a canine familiar with bear paws, a helper figure with vampirical requirements. For this need, Fursey has been provided with a supernumerary nipple, representing the only physical metamorphosis he undergoes after his ejection from Clonmacnoise. Albert may be a comic inversion of Fionn MacCumhaill's faithful hound Fermac, who could belch forth drink and treasures. While his presence may not be as useful, when Fursey eventually becomes despondent, having exiled himself to Britain after losing his beloved Maeve to Magnus, he abandons his Christian principles and feeds the familiar: "And then in the half-light of the cottage Fursey deliberately did evil for the first time in his life."[10]

Fursey has, up to this point, merely feigned acceptance of non-Christian characters and their beliefs. He humored the alleged sexton, Cuthbert, pretending to join the "brotherhood" of wizards in order to ecape to Clonmacnoise; he allowed a

sylphide to take his place in his cell in order to escape. The
only explanation Fursey may offer himself or Albert for this
unprecedented move is the desire to reclaim his lady love
(Maeve), to injure his competitor (Magnus), and to escape with
Maeve to a place of safety. Fursey's attitude changes, from resignation and little bravery to determination and courage, as
inspired by his attraction to a woman. Such a transformation
springs from *geis* violation and the breaking of whatever monastic vows he may still hold sacred. Because Fursey fails to
respect the taboo of the female, his life, like that of the pagan
hero, will be wrought with more havoc, and he will never be
able to reintegrate into the old order. The domestication of
Fursey and its disastrous consequences allow Wall to reinforce
the ecclesiastical satire, vis-à-vis fear of women. It also provides
for a comic depiction of the moonstruck and jealous lay
brother, who is ultimately unable to seek vengeance with full
malice, in the tradition of the cuckolded Conchobar (who ar-
ranges for Naoise's death, prompting Deirdre's suicide) or
Fionn MacCumhaill (who has Diarmaid killed in the boar
hunt). Wall again inverts Celtic heroic qualities, as Fursey actually befriends the competition.

That Mervyn Wall treats the female taboo with a light touch
is evident from the beginning of the first book. Father Furiosus
speaks with humility of the dangers of association with
women, while confessing past sins: "Thank God, I kept myself
free from the taint of women,"[11] the bishop later queries: "Did
it ever occur to you to wonder why God created women? It's
the one thing that tempts me at times to doubt His infinite
goodness and wisdom,"[12] and Father Furiosus laughs: "I never
knew a lying story that was not traceable to a woman."[13] It
takes the devil to explain why the clergymen's ignorance of the
nature of the female requires that he provide his figures of
temptation with exaggerated curvaceousness: "I've explained to
you till I'm worn out that the clergy's conception of women,
both physically and mentally, is a conception of something

which doesn't exist in this world."[14]

Fursey has clearly sinned against a greater interdiction, by adopting the powers of wizardry, before he commits the offense of romantic attachment. But this weakness connects the adventures of Fursey in love more plainly with old Celtic romance and legend, enhancing his satire and embellishing the comedy of both Fursey novels at the same time. In the first book, the Gray Mare's goat accidentally consumes a love potion, falling hopelessly in love with the hero. This comic adaptation of a motif from the King Mark legend (related to the Diarmaid and Grainne folktale) relates to the *ball seirce* or love spot device, which also occurs in the Fenian Grainne tale, excusing her somewhat for becoming enamored of Diarmaid. Wall uses this motif again in the second Fursey novel, in which the monk convinces his old friend Cuthbert to concoct a love philtre so that he may win back Maeve. Here, too, the results are comical rather than tragic; Fursey's cow consumes the entire bucket of potion. When Fursey studies the bovine face, he perceives the error: "There could be no doubt about it: the light in her eye was an amorous one."[15]

Any aspect of the Fursey novels that deals with nudity or sensuality is also designed for comic purposes, unlike many episodes in Celtic myth and legend. When Mugain and her ladies appear naked before Cuchulainn in a Ulidian tale, hoping to distract him from his threat to kill every man of Emain if he is not offered a combatant, the unclothed women operate in a serious manner. But when the naked sylphides harass the monks at Clonmacnoise, we are brought to laughter, as the frightened men scramble to escape and mortify the flesh, using nettles from the forest. And the pagan Celtic tradition of charging naked into battle is inverted through the christianized Irish aversion to nudity. King Cormac is censured for bathing nude in his tub; Fursey is literally defrocked or humiliated on more than one occasion.

In addition to this portrait of values that appear to reverse pre-Christian ones, Wall introduces historical allusions that point to the clergy's obsession with sacrilege and profanation. The setting of Clonmacnoise is appropriate, for his characters, like those from history, experience intimidation by woman-kind. In A.D. 842, the wife of a Viking raider apparently committed a taboo act by posturing herself on the Clonmac-noise altar and "giving oracles,"[16] and there is also a pagan Sheela-na-gig at Clonmacnoise. Defilement of an ostensible Christian center (with a pagan past, as evidenced in many early churches, which were built on the site of pre-Christian centers of worship) may be a source for Wall's devils' raid on the sanc-tuary once so strongly guarded by St. Keiran. It also reminds us of the constant struggle between the forces of pagan and Christian leaders, forces that operate in postconversion rendi-tions of Irish legends. Also, the Viking raids of this historical period provide a foundation for the heroic qualities Fursey will assume, even if they are somewhat lopsided.

Fursey relies on his powers of sorcery and good luck more than on bravery to secure safe passage from Mercia to Ireland on a Viking ship. Moreover, in joining forces with the enemy, albeit in the interest of self-preservation, Fursey again demon-strates inverted qualities of a traditional hero. Fionn MacCum-haill was said to defend Ireland from the Vikings, the false re-cording of which by Heinrich Zimmer caused Joyce to grant the hero Norse ancestry; Fursey nearly sells out his beloved homeland to the Northmen. But, turncoat at the last minute, for the lay brother never did intend the residents of Clonmac-noise any harm, he warns them in time to repel the attack.

While Hogan observes that the theme of the second book is sadder, for Fursey does indeed come very close to betraying the monastery and losing his soul,[17] those somber episodes are handled in a comic fashion. When Fursey fears that his fellow monks will perish, and Snorro, a "Christian Viking," a sarcas-tic juxtaposition of terms, assures him they will at least be with God that night, the hero replies: "I trust so. The only one I'd have any doubt about is the cook. He's a man of hard temper. Many the time when I was working with him in the kitchen he hit me over the head with the ladle; but, then, I suppose I wasn't much good."[18] When the devil arrives to claim Fursey's soul, the monk explains that he regurgitated the goatskin parchment on which he had signed his pledge to Satan. Even the loss of his beloved Maeve, despite a pact of friendship with Magnus and a mutual design for him to regain her, is treated with a humorous touch, particularly when juxtaposed against Celtic legends of unrequited love or acts of adultery. Magnus explains to his friend, apologetically, why he cannot "go off to war" and disappear. Their exchange is comitragic in tone; Fursey's naive responses cause an otherwise somber situation to border on the ridiculous. Magnus begins:

"She says that she's going to present me with a pledge of our love." Fursey gawked at Magnus with his mouth open. "Don't you understand, you clodpoll? She's going to present me with a squawker."

"Oh," said Fursey.

"I wouldn't be surprised if it's all on purpose. This is a woeful complication."

"I don't mind," said Fursey brightly. "I'll adopt it."

Magnus scowled at him. "Do you think I'd entrust my child to a ninnyhammer like you?"[19]

There is a sadness in the knowledge that Fursey, having seen the world, can no longer return to the monastic life, although the offer has been made. But Wall avoids a tragic endnote as Magnus concludes that Maeve, as all women, is now complete and most likely disdainful of both men. No battles are fought over the woman; no murders are committed; and Fursey's meek departure reminds us that he is no traditional warrior. Fursey lacks the suicidal excess of Cuchulainn and the lusty strength of Fionn MacCumhaill. But that is probably because, as a christianized Gaelic hero who consorts with nether-worldly figures, he is unable to rid himself of the spiritual qualities that were instilled in him during religious training. Fursey, unable to shed his humility and self-effacing qualities, cannot assert himself as a pagan Celtic hero and must remain suspended between the world of magic and the world of Christian hierarchy.

DARRELL FIGGIS: *THE RETURN OF THE HERO*

If the two Fursey novels satirize certain features of traditional writings, exposing shortcomings in the clerical milieu, but not offering any satisfactory alternatives in pagan worlds, there is an earlier work that celebrates the pre-Christian values of Fenian legend, and it does so for political and aesthetic reasons. Darrell Figgis published a novel entitled *The Return of the Hero* in 1923 under the pseudonym Michael Ireland (it was republished seven years later, posthumously, in New York, under his birth name). It is a brief novel that invokes a nostalgic yearning for the heroic qualities of Christian Ireland through a mixture of satire of the hypocrisy of the Irish Catholic clergy, of the comic naiveté of the legendary Oisin, and of the poetic glorification of nature. Figgis uses the framework of the medieval *Acallamh na Senorach*, the argument between St. Patrick and Oisin, converter and object of conversion, for this hero tale. He maintains the convention of the *seanachie* through Brogan, the scribe, in his history of the conflict between the aged pagan Gael and the self-righteous Galls. The Elders respect the leadership of Padraic macAlphurn (St. Patrick), although they tend to express independent views at different times in the proceedings; and the one Gaelic member of the *senorach*, Mac-Taill, is, along with St. Patrick, more sensitive to Oisin's plight, less rigid in his thinking, and receptive to the pre-Christian values of the *Fianna Eireann*.

The *fennid* Oisin, shown by Figgis to have returned to Ire-

land after two hundred years in the Land of the Young, is immediately recognizable as the hero of the Fenians. Said to come
from the West (Faeryland), Oisin is twice the height of any of
the twelve Elders and wears what was once colorful attire,
which brings to mind the biblical coat of motley: "Beneath the
tunic was a vest of many colors, all faded now like the dreams
of youthful splendor."[20]

But it becomes clear that more than Oisin's clothing has
faded; the heroic exploits of Fionn MacCumhaill his father,
Oscar his son, and Caoilte macRonan his comrade have paled
in the eyes of the converted Christians. It becomes Oisin's ob-
ligation to restore brightness to the old pagan ways; and Figgis
recaptures the brilliance through his character, becoming a
continuator of traditional Irish legends. The infamous Battle of
Gabhra, which Oisin mourns as the undoing of the *fennidi*,
becomes a standard of the strategies of honest warfare against
which the unscrupulous tactics of most of the Elders appear
contemptible. While Oisin is genuinely happy to entertain
them with accounts of the *Fianna*, not attempting to alter their
beliefs, the *Senorach* expect the one-time hero to let go of his
former ideals, submit to a ritual of baptism, and acknowledge
that the other members of the *fennidi* will burn in hell for
eternity.

Figgis portrays Oisin as a simple, guileless, and loyal hero
whose devotion to his family and comrades renders the expec-
tations of the Christians illogical and cruel. He presents St. Patrick's consternation over Fenian virtues and the paradox of
Fionn's damnation with a combination of humor and pathos.
Oisin, temporally and spatially removed from his tribe, initially perceives St. Patrick as a great druid. He refuses to genu-
flect before him or press his hands together in prayer because
this would, by Fenian convention, constitute an insult. "Oisin
had never seen men in that position, and it seemed to him that
there was something very offensive in their attitude. Their
hands, too, were placed palm to palm together, and held up in

front of their noses. It was a curious and insulting gesture, and Oisin could not explain it to himself."[21] We later learn that the Fenian also considered the act of forgiveness an offensive one because it implied condescension and amounted to vengeance. Oisin illustrates how contemptible forgiveness can be when he pronounces: "I forgive you all the breakfast I had this morning."[22]

While Oisin's plainspoken naiveté creates occasions for humor, it also creates moments of sadness. He must singlehandedly defend a moral code that, for him, is based on honesty and generosity, against a new morality that is rooted in mysticism and humility. Figgis accords much dignity to the great "Irish" saint, but his doctrine ultimately pales alongside the rules of conduct that guided Fionn and the *Fianna*. The ability of the earnest pagan to praise the strength and course of his own enemy is no longer virtuous; physical prowess is deemed inferior to mortification of the body. "If it was hard to get a man to see that truth was only a virtue when it was a fruit of faith, it was still harder to get him to learn that health and robustness were signs of decay and corruption."[23] Oisin explains that, to the *fennidi*, desires of the body were not devils; and he confesses to Bishop Auxilius that he is ignorant of "sin." This notion appears in Mervyn Wall's first Fursey novel, where, as has been noted, a wizard explains that the devil was an invention of Christianity.

If we allow that pagan Celtic *geasa* can be translated into Christian sins, Oisin underscores the difference between the two types of trangressions, explaining that *geis* breaking constitutes an offense against oneself with immediate and tangible repercussions, rather than a trespass against God with eternal accountability. He provides an example of pagan *geis* when he explains that, upon his return from Tir na nOg, his feet were never to touch the ground, nor was he to alight from his steed. Breaking the *geasa*, which he did out of impulsive generosity, assisting in the lifting of a stone, causes physical threat rather than spiritual harm.

But if the concept of sin is foreign to Oisin, then the notion of original sin is even more difficult to understand. As a proponent of active heroism, the pagan warrior cannot grasp the idea that he has passively inherited the great sin of mankind. Because Oisin logically dismisses his father's need for baptism, Fionn having existed in an age before the knowledge of original sin had even been imparted to the Irish, he cannot understand why MacCumhaill is not partaking of the joys of the heaven that St. Patrick describes. And Oisin's perception of heaven itself is one of more connectedness to the physical world. He states simply: "The portals of earth are the gates of heaven."[24] This is only one of several pronouncements that infuriate most of the Elders, but it sways MacTaill (a character who has already begun to confuse Ulidian tales with Fenian ones and pagan poems with Christian prayers) toward defense of the pagan. Figgis carefully separates the small-mindedness of the bishops from the precepts of the new religion, yet he allows Oisin to function as a symbol of the old faith. The artful rhetoric of Auxilius and the "vision" of Iserninus are no match against Oisin's wisdom. The pagan hero remains confident in his ideology because he has witnessed firsthand the Fenian thumb of knowledge in action, and he can testify personally to the hospitality of his father, whereas the Elders rely on hearsay and pure faith for their convictions. Oisin is completely lacking in motive and desires only to be reunited with his old band. The *Senorach*, however, base their argument on faith in that which they have not seen and operate on the principle that they have to determine who has achieved salvation and who has not. They scarcely disguise their anxiousness to eliminate the Fenians from the rosters of heaven; with cunning they nearly overpower St. Patrick.

The final determination of Oisin's fate and the status of Fionn is made only after the ancient hero and St. Patrick have conducted, or reenacted, the famous debate or contest between

their two personal heroes, Fionn MacCumhaill and Jesus
Christ. Oisin insists that heroes be compared in light of their
deeds, for, as he explains: "It is the man of guile who speaks in
council of consequences."[25] Patrick cleverly relates a strong
example of Christian heroism, choosing the parable of a warrior Christ driving the merchants out of the temple and another tale of generosity, using the parable of the loaves and the
fishes, both of which appeal to the *fennid*. But his line of argument angers Oisin when he speaks of Christian charity,
which the latter considers as debasing as forgiveness. Oisin is
also suspicious of the memory-eradicating properties of baptism, a rite that implies remorse for past deeds and that brings
up a sentiment for which Oisin sees no purpose. The forthright pagan, whose longing to see Fionn is much stronger than
any desire to approach God, finally recites a tale of his father's
deeds in order to guide the Elders in their decision concerning
his soul's fate. Having needlessly memorized numerous precepts of Christianity, under Brogan's tutelage Oisin's final test
is not one of knowledge but of proving the sanctity of the *fennidi*. Figgis has placed the hero in the Elders' court, where he
agrees to play by their rules, but he provides him with the skill
of reciting Fenian traditional legend and strengthens the satire
through his superior narrative technique.

Oisin displays enthusiasm in his rendition of the tale he has
selected, that of the magical cup, silencing Seachnall's interrup-
tion that hints at the sin of adultery with a fitting rejoinder:
"Men do not see other men but through their own eyes. One
man's idea of another man's character is the best expression of
his own."[26] Padraic macAlphurn happily finds allusions to the
Holy Grail (as do folklorists) in the magical cup story, fer-
vently hoping to declare Fionn saved. But his interpretations
are rejected by the other bishops, who refuse to entertain the
idea of Fionn enjoying the promise of heaven.

When Oisin eventually learns of his father's unfortunate
fate, Figgis interrupts the narration to offer authorial com-

ments on the textual variants of the *Acallamh na Senorach* with respect to Oisin's outrage. Despite the abruptness of the strategy, the poetic quality of Oisin's speech and his reverence for nature are restored. Prior to his magical disappearance, Oisin expresses his love of Ireland and its ancient heroes:

> We are one where we have loved. We will rove
> the pleasant places. We will hear the pleasant sounds.
> The wave of Rughraidhe lashing the shore, the lowing
> of oxen in Maghmaoin, the seagull's scream in distant
> Iorrus. The murmur of streams on Sliabh Mis,
> the yell of the hounds at Drumlis, the noise of the
> fasons around Sliabh gCua. The hound's deep bay
> at twilight's fall and the barque's sharp grating on the
> shore. We are they, they are we, O captain. We are
> where we have loved.[27]

In light of his allegiance to the old ways, Oisin's disappearance must take him back to the soil of pre-Christian Ireland, where he may reunite with his people. Figgis follows the hero's mysterious departure with tales of visions and wonders. He situates a Christian procession, druidic at first appearance, in his own birthplace, Gleann-na-Smol. At this site, a Catholic church is not to be built because its cornerstone was laid by a pagan. The superstitious caution, which saddens St. Patrick and MacTaill, provides another occasion for a pessimistic author's indictment of the Elders, who may stand for modern Ireland. The stone, deemed a memory of Oisin, renews the Fenian Cycle in its tribute to the pagan hero; Figgis himself, sadly, died by suicide two years after publishing *The Return of the Hero*.

NOTES

1. Robert Hogan, *Mervyn Wall* (Lewisburg, Pa.: Bucknell University Press, 1972), p. 9.

2. Gordon Henderson, "An Interview with Mervyn Wall," *Journal of Irish Literature* 11, no. 1 (1982), p. 7.

3. Vladimir Propp, *Morphology of the Folktale*, 2nd ed. (1958; rpt. Austin: University of Texas Press, 1968), p. 30.

4. Mervyn Wall, *The Unfortunate Fursey* (London: Pilot Press, 1946), p. 12.

5. Hogan, *Mervyn Wall*, p. 37.

6. Patrick C. Power, *A Literary History of Ireland* (Cork: Mercier Press, 1969), p. 26.

7. Vivian Mercier, *The Irish Comic Tradition* (Oxford: Oxford University Press, 1962), p. 173.

8. *The Unfortunate Fursey*, p. 98.

9. Ibid., 133.

10. Mervyn Wall, *The Return of Fursey* (London: Pilot Press, 1948), p. 24.

11. *The Unfortunate Fursey*, p. 28.

12. Ibid., p. 41.

13. Ibid., p. 46.

14. Ibid., p. 141.

15. *The Return of Fursey*, p. 174.

16. Frank Delaney, *The Celts* (Boston: Little, Brown, and Co., 1986), p. 54.

17. Robert Hogan, "Mervyn Wall," in *Supernatural Fiction Writers: Fantasy and Horror*, vol. 2, ed. E. F. Bleiler (New York: Charles Scribner's Sons, 1985), p. 649.

18. *The Return of Fursey*, pp. 80-81.

19. Ibid., pp. 232-233.

20. Michael Ireland, *The Return of the Hero* (London: Chapman and Dodd., 1923), p. 16.

21. Ibid., p. 24.

22. Ibid., p. 127.

23. Ibid., p. 76.

24. Ibid., p. 99.

25. Ibid., p. 122.

26. Ibid., p. 184.

27. Ibid., p. 240.

CHAPTER 6

Eimar O'Duffy: A Satirical Trilogy

How to Have Money Always

Kill a black cock, and go to the meeting of three cross-roads where a murderer is buried. Throw the dead bird over your left shoulder then and there, after nightfall, in the name of the devil, holding a piece of money in your hand all the while. And ever after, no matter what you spend, you will always find the same piece of money undiminished in your pocket.[1]

An old ritual, recorded by Lady Wilde, illustrates an early Irish pragmatic concern for financial security. The key word of the formula is "undiminished," for there is no concern expressed over growth, compound interest, or wealth at the expense of others. It is the antithesis of this simple desire for economic stability that Eimar O'Duffy satirizes in his trilogy *King Goshawk and the Birds* (1926), *The Spacious Adventures of the Man in the Street* (1928), and *Asses in Clover* (1933). O'Duffy's narrative technique has been likened to that of Thomas More, Jonathan Swift, and George Bernard Shaw, all of whom write of dystopic and utopic worlds. But O'Duffy's particular use of elements from Ireland's mythical and legendary heroic age adds a new dimension to the meaning of satire.

O'Duffy's dystopia, the modern age, is not the bane of christianization, as hinted at in other Irish literary works. We are not limited to the viewpoint of one suffering individual, such as Mervyn Wall's Fursey, who might have fared better in the pre-Christian period. Instead, O'Duffy casts Evil, in the manner of a morality play, in the role of twentieth-century (or later) advanced capitalism, and he features the proletarians of this planet as victims of an economic system. The only hope for the world is in a return to tradi ional Irish heroic values, some of which include the romantic notions of bravery, loyalty, and justice, in the code of Cuchulainn and his warriors. While races other than the Celts have their own heroic traditions and cultural wellsprings, the Celtic sagas, with which O'Duffy was probably most familiar, are highly suitable for purposes of contrast with the modern age.

The evil of capitalism's monopolies and overproduction of commodities, which create poverty and starvation, are presented immediately in Part One of the trilogy, *King Goshawk and the Birds*. But the opening pillow talk scene between the futuristic Wheat King, Goshawk, and his greedy wife, Guzzelinda, does more than mimic the beginning of the Irish epic *Tain*, as noted by Robert Hogan.[2] It confers the role of chief villain on an American tycoon, one who lives across the sea. In the Fenian Cycle, the *fomoire*, or evil, piratical invaders came from similarly removed lands. Thus O'Duffy writes: "now shift we our ground to the city of Dublin, between the sea and the mountains, by the bright waters of Liffey; where our feet tread more easily than on the shores of Manhattan or in the palaces of kings."[3]

Dublin, the anagrammatic Bulnid and center of Rathean (Earthan) civilization in the second part of O'Duffy's trilogy, is hardly the locus of perfection. Yet it is closer in spirit and in miles to the only source of hope in the advanced age of objectivisms, the locus for the resurrection of Cuchulainn and his begetting of a son on earth. And, like many modern Irish writers who blend pagan and Christian values, O'Duffy writes of a "Second Coming" and situates the scene for such an event in a humble environment. It is in the impoverished conditions of the district of Stoneybatter that a philosopher, Murphy, learns about the fulfillment of Goshawk's wife's outrageous request, the acquisition of all the world's songbirds. This philosopher is relegated to the Third Heaven, or Tir na nOg, by Socrates, whom he encounters in the Twentieth Heaven, a setting deemed too lofty for his purposes, the retrieval of the songbirds. He is eventually assisted by a simple Irish grocer's assistant, Robert Emmet Aloysius O'Kennedy, who allows Cuchulainn to inhabit his body so that he may roam the earth (the word thereby becoming flesh). O'Duffy cleverly sends O'Kennedy's soul into space, which provides for the plot of Part Two of the trilogy, *The Spacious Adventures of the Man in the Street*. But before "metamorphosis" can be attained, O'Duffy lingers nostalgically on the age of the Ulidian Cycle and the nobility of the hero's spirit:

In those days, said the mind of the Philosopher, men fought with men in hot blood, hand to hand, strength against strength, feet against feet, and knowing well what it was they were fighting for. But for many centuries they have been possessed of a devilish powder which enables them to kill at a distance; and by labouring hard at its improvement they have learnt how to kill without seeing one another at all.[4]

The Philosopher goes on to bemoan the passing of the fair fight and to describe the horrors of bombs and nerve gas, the writer's reflections on innovations of World War I; and some of his musings remind us of Darrell Figgis' resurrected Oisin, who cannot understand how modern man fails to respect the prowess of his enemy. The Philosopher's supplications to Cuchulainn, however, do not provoke a reaction until he speaks of Goshawk's usurpation of the songbirds. The warrior hero's affinity for nature's bounty and his conviction that it must be shared by all men spur him to action. O'Duffy implies that advancing materialism represents modern man's greatest deviation from traditional values, although this thirst for ownership spawns even greater evils.

Cuchulainn's shock and dismay at the degeneration of modern Irish civilization provide for comic satire as well as bitter condemnation of modern values. O'Duffy abandons much of the lightness by the time he composes the third part of his trilogy, for purposes of moralizing, perhaps. But the satire may prove more appealing and effective through scenes such as the one in which Cuchulainn reveals his hero halo and undergoes frightening physical distortions after a shopkeeper insists that he pay for his food. The hero simply cannot grasp man's desire for profit when supplying a basic need. The Philosopher is forced to lay thematic *geasa* upon Cuchulainn, "that for no cause whatsoever, should he strike or otherwise mishandle any human being, or any property of any human being whatsoever."[5]

As may be expected, Cuchulainn goes on to violate other, unwritten laws that did not exist in the time of myth and legend. One of these is the taboo of straightforward sexual propositions; and Cuchulainn, in all naiveté, shamelessly blunders in a conversation with a woman whom he finds attractive:

My desire is for two snowy mountains, rose-crowned that are fenced along with thorns and barriers of ice. What shall I do to melt the ice and turn aside the menace of thorns?

What do you mean? asked the maiden.

Then, said Cuchulainn, it is your bare bosom that is the fruit of my desiring, and your red lips ripe for kissing, and your warm white body to be pressed in mine in the clasp of love.

O you dirty fellow! cried the girl, and turning, she fled into her house.[6]

The bardic tradition of metaphor and the directness of the hero's appeal are either misunderstood or rejected, and when

the Censors attempt to jail Cuchulainn when he openly admits
he has no intentions of marriage, he is forced to break his *geasa*
and tie the arresting officers literally in knots.

When the Philosopher convinces the disgusted hero to remain a while longer on earth and sire a heroic son who will
free the birds, we see that economics rules all decisions. The
sage advises Cuchulainn to select, as a breeder, a young mil-
lionairess, who is likely to be most beautiful, having the skin
and body that gentility permits or money can buy. There is no
facet of human existence that has not been shaped, to some degree, by modern economics, and Cuchulainn accepts this fact
when he kidnaps Thalia, the daughter of tycoon Boodleguts.

O'Duffy does, however, situate the scene of conception and
birth of the heroic child beyond the earthly realm. Cuandine,
who springs forth in the Tir na nOg, comes into the world
with all the peculiarities that traditionally surround heroes in
Celtic lore and universal legends. He possesses five years'
worth of knowledge from the womb, extraordinary strength,
and the gift of poetry. Cuandine's curse of three faults—
disobedience (the Adam Complex), lying (the Ulysses Complex), and curiosity about women (the Gynaecothaumastic Li-
bido)—combines the sacred Celtic triad with the Christian trinity, superstitious and biblical theory, and Freudian psychol-
ogy. The author provides him with the traditional heroic
macgnimartha or training period, during which time he is sent
to the Heaven of the Idealists and the Heaven of the Realities,
by age ten, when manhood is reached. When he finally de-
scends to earth, Cuandine assumes his mission or injunction of
freeing the songbirds, returning us to O'Duffy's satire of capi-
talist evils. As Vivian Mercier observes, the author, exaggerat-
ing the ills of the modern age, presents evils in a futuristic time
that do not differ in kind but in degree.[7]

Thus Cuandine learns about the functions of the newspaper,
which include devoting disproportionate space to meaningless
social trivia and granting near equal coverage to the

"sportsmanship" of one Lord Puddlehead, who felled more than a million birds, and the ongoing Wolfo-Lambian War. The aggressive modern woman is also developed to an extreme, as Cuandine wrestles with the attentions of a stream of women and manifests a naiveté that parallels his father's attitude. His honesty is comical as he plays the ingénu:

I hope, said Cuandine, that they will all fall in love with me, as I have with them.
But surely, said the Philosopher, you must see that will bring torment and heartbreak among them?
No, faith, said Cuandine; for I will deny myself to none of them.[8]

Cuandine's failure to appreciate human jealousy redirects the reader to the philosophy of the heroic age, when magnanimity ruled in love, and possessiveness was akin to ownership of the sky or the green grass. Further, Cuandine must learn that honesty is not necessarily a sign of wisdom in the modern age. He must conceal his true emotions, just as recording his actual birthdate or parentage would cause him to be taken for insane.

O'Duffy depicts a true portrait of insanity through his painting of Dublin, where successful entrepreneurs inhabit mansions, and the gateway to the homes of the millionaires hold a sign stating: "What we have we hold." Cuandine eventually leaves Ireland, to tour the world by airbus, after receiving the financial backing he requires from a 106-year-old millionaire named MacWhelahan, to whom he reveals the secret that there really is no hell. The old man's response to the revelation, while an honest one, points out how individual greed, taken to an extreme, leads to charitable acts performed as a sort of insurance against eternal punishment:

Oh, well, who wants to enter the kingdom of heaven anyway?— so long as the other place isn't the alternative, I mean. You know, prophet, I wish I'd met you a bit earlier. When I think of all the

money I've wasted on charities, churches, schools, convents, and the
Lord knows what—to say nothing of the business opportunities I've
let slip on account of my conscientious scruples—well, it pretty well
gets my goat.⁹

Cuandine discovers that those who serve Mammon are not
restricted to Ireland and that social inequities, vivisection, and
the failure of the legal system are but some of the atrocities ob-
servable the world over. However, Ireland is the site of his
proposed reform, and Cuandine returns to Dublin, resolved to
enter the political scene and rouse the people into seeking justice. In frustration, he confesses his identity to the Irish (*geis*
violation), only to find himself a subject of ridicule in an
authorial rendering that resembles recordings of the New Testament in which Christ's identity is challenged.

Courted by two competitive newspaper tycoons, Lords
Mammoth and Cumbersome, Cuandine temporarily succumbs
to temptation as he seeks recognition in England. But we never
lose sight of his heroic status when financial proposals are
made, particularly when Lord Mammoth's greed surfaces:

The danger star glowed in Cuandine's eye at that, and the whirr
of the gathering of the Bocanachs and the Bacanachs sounded in the
distance like the first whisper of a coming storm. The Philosopher,
mindful of how they used to treat Cuchulainn in such crises, threw
over him a jugful of water. I will not say that it boiled as it fell from
his body (though indeed it did), for you would not believe me; but
we have Lord Mammoth's testimony that a splash of it scalded him
through his trousers, and certain it is that two more jugs were
needed to reduce the hero's temperature to normal.¹⁰

If this does not serve as a warning that the English expedition will be a failure, we should note the author's intrusion
into the discussion with respect to his neighbors: "Now, as
every Irishman knows, the people of England are in every way
inferior to the people of Ireland, being materialists, whereas we
are idealists."¹¹ The statement may sum up the philosophy of

the first book of O'Duffy's trilogy, for the indictment of materialism is only meaningful when objectivist values are juxtaposed against those of a more symbolic nature. The observation also explains why the British newspapers report details of Ulidian folklore in a strictly literal fashion, speaking of "Mr. Coondinner's father" (Cuchulainn) as a "noted athlete" and of the naming of "Cu Hoolin" as one of many "quaint Irish customs." The materialists relate only to objective facts. When Cuandine realizes that he no longer holds novelty value for the British, and can do little to change the economic persuasion of the modern age, he injects himself into the Wolfo-Lambian War. In this pursuit, Cuandine tries to restore the notion of fair play, in the style of combat inherent in Irish myth. Refusing guns, Cuandine avails himself of only his father's sword, the Cruaidin Cailidcheann, and sets up battle between twenty of the best men from each side. The battle strategy is mapped out only after the hero first attempts to establish peace, as Cuchulainn had once sought to convince his foster brother Ferdia not to engage in combat with him. Cuandine has no choice left him but to vanquish the Wolfians, demanding his terms as the Morrigu appear above his head. He paralyzes the Wolfians with fear and humiliates their dictator Nervolini with a walloping before his own people. The somewhat contrived Marchen-style conclusion to this book would preclude continuation of the satire were it not for the disembodied spirit of O'Kennedy, which must reappear and find its way back to earth.

In *The Spacious Adventures of the Man in the Street*, O'Duffy apparently puts aside Celtic structural and thematic devices as he develops plot, yet they intrude in a more subtle way. The outer body experiences of Robert Emmet Aloysius O'Kennedy surpass those of Swift's Gulliver. O'Duffy not only introduces an earthling into an alien society, but also divides him into a two-part metamorphosed figure who inhabits the shell of a recently executed Rathean citizen and the soul of the quintessential Irish workingman, who mentally maintains communication with his earthly employer, Mr. Gallagher. Just as Celtic gods and heroes can change shape while retaining their identities, so O'Kennedy assumes the physical body of Ydenneko (which sounds suspiciously like "identical") while continuing to communicate O'Kennedy's reactions to the reader. Further, in his time- and space-transcending travel and exposure to the prudish, avaricious, dishonest, and cruel practices of the "aliens," or Ratheans, we recognize the antithesis of Celtic heroic values. The sexual inhibitions of earthlings, for example, are satirized via the Ratheans' repressed attitudes toward food.

Rathean priorities are generally based on aesthetic appeal, and the pragmatism of objectivist philosophy is rendered meaningless. O'Duffy transcends socialist treatise in this work and calls for a return to a lifestyle that is more closely attuned to nature and beauty. Individuals have only original paintings in their homes rather than cheap (bourgeois) reproductions; and O'Kennedy learns that only painting, music, and poetry rank above gardening in Rathe. Rathean culture restores what is held to be of paramount importance in traditional writings and what modern society classifies as leisure activity.

Rathean children, unhampered by the financial restrictions of modern civilization, develop rapidly, much like the heroes Cuchulainn and Fionn MacCumhaill. O'Kennedy learns that "in Rathe children could walk and talk when they were born, and (that) some could even sing or play the piano. At a year old they could read and write; at two they went to school; and at seven they were grown men and women."[12] Ratheans are additionally enlightened in their disdain for money and gold (as Thomas More's Raphael observes Utopians laughing at gold ornaments); and they use precious metal to make street lamps. In a later adventure, Ianda explains, "You can do anything with savages by throwing them baksheesh,"[13] as she tosses gold overboard and saves O'Kennedy's life. Like Cuchulainn, who was stirred up into one of his metamorphoses in *King Goshawk and the Birds* when asked to pay for food, O'Kennedy, who has grown unaccustomed to the use of money, nearly gets himself in trouble when billed for a meal at a restaurant on Tiger's Island, a penal colony of Rathe.

The Ratheans value honor and trust above all possessions, and their vocabulary contains no word for prison or punishment. Idleness is deemed worse than murder; distrust, a burden. As Rathean Ytteb explains: "a distrustful mind is a heavy weapon to carry about. I'd sooner wear armor."[14] Their code of honor guarantees women equal rights while recognizing marriage and children as a full time job, a need for personal privacy, and the value of a liberal education. The Ratheans astound O'Kennedy because they possess no moral code and are completely devoid of jealousy.

The Rathean issue of "morality" revolves around attitudes toward food, as mentioned earlier, rather than toward sex; thus they practice what is almost a religious form of monophagy. Eating is taboo for discussion, and the term "hunger" is euphemized to "taste," just as "love" is often substituted for "lust." O'Duffy creates a satire of human attitudes toward sex via his illicit eating parlors, trials to change the food choice to which Ratheans are wedded for life, a food liberation movement known as "Free Eats," and even the notion of a confessional novel, *A Picture of My Youth*, in which a youth craves food before the age of seven, and which, of course, recalls Joyce's *Portrait of the Artist as a Young Man*. O'Kennedy refuses to mate, unwedded, with Ytteb, as there is no priest on Rathe to forgive the "sin," at which point O'Duffy introduces a contrast with the Celtic hero's guilt-free atttitude regarding sexual union and the convention of *geis*, in that Rathean culture requires some type of interdiction. Violation of the *geis* carries the same stigma as it would in traditional folklore, a loss of social standing which explains why the chief's son, Ensulas, who befriends O'Kennedy, must visit eating houses on the

sneak. When Professor Juicewit calls the earthling's eating habits "hideous debauchery" and "an orgy of gluttonous enjoy-
ment," he emphasizes a need for taboo.

If O'Duffy creates a race with an unusual social framework
on Rathe, he also bestows on them an unusual religion. The
Ratheans are Diabologians, or devil-worshipers, who practice a
faith called Procrusteanity. Mercier feels that O'Duffy deliberately chooses a religion that exactly opposes Christianity to
show that, as the Ratheans practice their faith just about as se-
riously as Christians practice theirs, no harm can come of it.[15]
Its name also curiously echoes Christianity, when pronounced
phonetically, underscoring the possible similarities between
the two.

However, there is an added dimension to the religion of
darkness, or Positivism, of Rathe, and that is the alien's dread
of eternal life. This, again, recalls the Celtic concept of Tir na
nOg, which is neither heaven nor hell, but a tangible, pastoral
place of existence for gods and heroes, from which they may
return to Ireland at will. The safety of the materiality in the
sidhe, or fairy mounds, beneath which spirits dwell, or the de-
scendants of the Tuatha de Danaan hide, arises from a closer
bond to earth. Christianized abodes of eternal punishment or
reward stymied Oisin in the *Acallamh*, for the finality of the
suffering or joy does not suit Celtic cosmology. Infinity is too
long a time to pay for one's misdeeds.

O'Duffy calls for a reinstatement of fairness and justice in
man's earthly life and illustrates man's potential for cruelty
through an inverted Rathean hunting ritual. When wild animals are set after men, O'Kennedy remarks, "The sight of a
fellow man torn to pieces ought to horrify anybody," to which
Ytteb responds: "Well yes. It was a pity he didn't get away. But
wasn't it a splendid run?"[16] O'Duffy recalls a code whereby
hunting was performed for purposes of survival, whether to
secure food or fulfill an injunction, and not just for sport. The
Rathean game of setting traps for humans underscores the im-

balances in human activities and the disappearance of fair play.

O'Kennedy's heroic journey, out of the Sunny Zone, and into the Eastern and Western Shady Zones, the Twilight Zone, and, finally, the Dark Zone, reveals, like Cuandine's world tour, many instances of cruelty and injustice. As in the first book of the trilogy, Ireland (here Bulnid) may be bad, but things do not get any better beyond its borders. Traveling through space and time with the exiled Kwashog (or Goshawk), formerly vice-president of Rathe's Chamber of Commerce, O'Kennedy discovers the mutilated race of Outlanders on the Dark Side of the planet. The underlings of the race, slaves of the Harpaxeans, are subjected to a removal of their tibia at birth, in order to fit into their undersized dwellings, which stand twelve to fifteen feet high. When O'Kennedy requests an explanation for their surgical dwarfing of these people, he first receives an argument based on economic realities, a lack of building materials: "Life in these regions" (Kwashog explained) "is based on common sense and economic facts, not on the romantic theories that flourish in the sunshine. Did you notice these peoples' legs? Not pretty, are they? Well, they weren't born like that. They get them shortened artificially by removing the shin bones in infancy."[17] But further explanation reveals that the Harpaxeans, residents of the capital of the Black Lands, had, for several generations, undergone "all sorts of mutilations for the sake of appearance or fashion." Because custom and convention have long ago removed man's appreciation of "romantic" necessities and reduced his life to material concerns, it is not surprising that his physical appearance undergo modifications for economic pragmatism. The traditional Celtic obsession with physical beauty is thus inverted; mutations are started in the name of progress.

A related passage that deals with canines imbued with the enterprising spirit of human merchants (thanks to the transplanting of servants' brains into their heads, which also permits mindless servants) points to further disruption in modern soci-

ety. The near sacred role of the hound in the Fenian Cycle is
obscured through the cloning procedures of servants and dogs.
Fionn's dog Bran was, like his master, endowed with a remarkable degree of foreknowledge of evil and could therefore
warn Fionn of imminent danger.[18] The farcical "Mr." Towser,
a liberated spaniel with his own rat-catching business, whom
O'Kennedy has befriended, laments the canine theory of evolution. The emancipated animal, unbalanced by his brain-grafting
procedure, is doomed to exist halfway between two worlds.
Referring to wolves as possible ancestors, he denies that his
race could have sprung from creatures "so brutal and debased."
He claims that "certain physical resemblances" misled anthro-
pologists into proposing this theory; interestingly, his objec-
tions are not based on religious controversy but canine pride.
O'Duffy spoofs the human-simian theory of evolution
through an appropriate character choice, one who has severed
all ties with nature and lost the dignity he was accorded in traditional Irish hero tales.

But even the hero of this adventure, O'Kennedy, must sacrifice his dignity as he completes his tour of the hellish Dark
Side. O'Kennedy is, after all, the soul of a modern Irishman in
the body of a dead Rathean, therefore not endowed with the
peculiarities of Irish mythological heroes. An appeal to his ego
persuades him to take charge of an army that would make war
against Rathe, and the simple man soon revels in the glory of
his command. He becomes involved in a full-scale military
drama that calls for the use of heavy artillery and poison gas,
the very weapons whose use had appalled Cuchulainn in *King
Goshawk and the Birds*. O'Kennedy, a failure in the Middle
Zone, finds himself in a Kafkaesque setting, in which he is examined for the purpose of classifying him as man or ape:

Their researches had been mainly conducted into our mental and
physiological characteristics; and on this basis the evidence was un-
certain, confused, and contradictory. Our quarrelsomeness, ferocity,
vindictiveness, and general love of mischief were markedly simian

indicators, as were our acquisitive-ness, our mania for collecting use-
less things, our vanity, our addiction to meaningless chatter, our
gluttony, and our irrational taboos.[19]

O'Kennedy is eventually declared more human than ape (in
a close call), found guilty of conspiring against world peace,
and sentenced to be shot the next morning. O'Kennedy, by
abandoning his role of observer and attempting to implement
earth values in Rathe, has violated an interdiction.

In Joyce's epic novels, Bloom and Earwicker stand trial for
implied personal transgressions; in O'Brien's first two novels,
his heroes suffer from acute paranoia and must pay for their
sins of power mongering and murder; in Wall's fantasies, Fursey unwittingly consorts with the devil; and Figgis' resurrected Fionn stands trial (defended by his son) for the deeds of
the *fianna*. But the hero of O'Duffy's second novel in the trilogy has broken *geis* simply by challenging Rathean views and
is declared "a dangerous person whose continued existence is a
menace to the peace of the world."[20] He is, therefore, executed.

Naturally, they can only execute the physical half of
O'Kennedy, because, as a Christian, he would believe in the
immortality of his soul. He takes this second "death" in his
stride, even anticipating a third one, and gives up his body as
willingly as he once did for the Philosopher in order to lend it
to Cuchulainn. O'Kennedy's soul wanders through space and
encounters many forms of "god," ranging from the loathsome
Moloch to a god of Love and Beauty, who, like the modern
woman Zip of the Dark Zone, advocates an exploitative, *carpe
diem* philosophy. And, when the Devil challenges the existence
of any god at all, O'Kennedy is remanded to Murphy the Philosopher and returned to a body that Cuchulainn has stretched
out of shape. Because the deeds of mortal O'Kennedy are no
match for the exploits of the Celtic hero of myth, this division
of the trilogy ends as the "Second part of the comical epic," as
opposed to O'Duffy's closing of Part One, which he calls the
"ancient epic tale of the deeds of Cuandine." O'Kennedy has

witnessed the inversion and negation of many traditions, but all he can do is repeat the errors of modern man.

The intervention of the gods alone can set things right on earth again, so Cuandine must reappear in the third novel of O'Duffy's trilogy, *Asses in Clover*. But, as Robert Hogan comments, the satire is not as effective in this last volume, for it is simply too blatant.[21] If the author resorts to pedantry in the face of a world depression, he still offers lighter moments of inspiration through the introduction of a new character, Mac ui Rudai. This humble human has simple habits and needs that recall a mythical (or at least, pre-industrial) age. Unfortunately, he expresses them in an increasingly complex world, in which, as we may expect from O'Duffy, economic imperatives determine each aspect of human existence. Mac ui Rudai does not have the same total despondence of early O'Kennedy, who willingly surrenders his body because he has lost the will to go on. When Mac ui Rudai encounters Cuandine, who is now traveling the world on foot because he is broke, he is described as "a good fellow after his fashion but somewhat wild and barbarous and rather lewd in his habits. He would eat when he was hungry, drink when he was thirsty, and preferred wine to water when he could afford it; besides which he was of a mind to marry when he fell in love, and embrace his wife under the promptings of passion."[22]

These practices and desires run counter to the new philosophy, which is not founded on logic. Hence St. Progressa becomes the prophylactic patroness of women, and men drop to the ground and prostrate themselves before a banker. When Mac ui Rudai is run over by a car, the citizens declare him "superfluous" and throw him into jail. O'Duffy not only exaggerates the reverses of traditional values, but also restates his indignation over the disappearance of the *fili* or seeker poet. In *The Spacious Adventures of the Man in the Street*, he had introduced the problem of the dearth of quality writing through the notion of writing out texts by hand in the Middle Zone.

O'Kennedy is told that so little valuable literature is generated that mechanized publication methods are not required. In *Asses in Clover*, O'Duffy mourns the passing of the bardic tradition, as a bookseller tells Cuandine:

> You must understand that the poet does not use words for their meaning, but for their emotive resonance. He treats language as a piano, not a dictionary—twists words about to make them more significant, runs them together so as to blend their meaning, uses prepositions and conjunctions, freely—much as a composer uses drumtaps and cuts loose from syntax altogether.[23]

Thanks to this style of composition, novels are turned out by mass production. Heavy advertising costs make it impossible to publish a good book. And perhaps O'Duffy addresses the critics through the words of Mr. Pewling Mush, the uplift writer of the Cumbersome Press: "I am not accustomed to interruptions. They break the free flow of my argument. Nobody ever interrupts my articles. They must be taken as a whole, without plucking phrases out of their context."[24]

The best writing of this age may be propaganda, and O'Duffy evidently feels justified in doling out a bit of his own as he becomes increasingly didactic. Even Cuandine, who has learned the art of unscrupulousness in the fourth heaven, is prepared to compose propaganda for the war between Assinaria and Farawavia. This "war to end war" sees the corruption of Mac ui Rudai, who invents nerve gas and is subsequently honored as a humanitarian. His *bean a'tighe*, the seventeen-year-old bride, Kathrynne, turns out a disappointment, for she lets their baby die from neglect and deserts her husband out of boredom. When the dejected Mac ui Rudai turns to Cuandine for moral support and the world appears lost to all hope, O'Duffy reintroduces the heroic mode of existence.

The author had physically removed Cuchulainn from the material world, one ruled by bank director Slawmy Cander and Wheat King Goshawk, in order for the son of Lugh to be-

get Cuandine through his union with Thalia. This time
Cuandine needs to distance himself from the trappings of human existence, and he unites with a girl who gives him "the
seven pleasures of women." O'Duffy's reintroduction to the
heroic world resembles a hymn to wedded bliss. Angus Og
explains Cuandine's need to sleep for seven years, while his
wife bears two sons, who, "as befitting the offspring of heroes,"
grow in a week as ordinary children do in a year. The twins are
educated by Cuchulainn, Sencha, Bricriu, Cathbad, Ferdiad,
Naoise, Ainnle and Ardan, and Fergus. Because his sons are
three-quarters human (as are the twin girls they later bear),
Cuandine worries over their sexual desires and counsels them
"that they should be the masters, not the slaves, of their appe-
tites, and that they should rather forego all pleasures than to do
anything unseemly for the sake of it."[25] The pastoral quality of
the idyllic passage underlies concern with the false moral and
distorted values of the industrialized world. Cuandine must,
however, return to this world if he is finally to rescue the birds
from Goshawk and, upon returning, discovers that one of the
queen's birds has escaped. The creature has been granted protection in Ireland, suggesting an affinity for the oppressed who
are released from slavery. A full-scale war ensues, in the tradition of the *Tain bo Cuailgne*, on an international scale. Battle is
done, ostensibly for the repossession of nature's bounty; in
reality, the principle of ownership or control is at stake. The
Irish stalwartly refuse to return the blackbird, possibly representing their resistance to power mongering and monopoliza-
tion. But, were it not for the intervention of Cuandine, their
noble cause would crumble because of internal disunity.
O'Duffy interjects the curse of the Celtic god Crom Cruach
upon the Irish: "that whenever an enemy should attack them,
and their need of unity be greatest, then should division and
hatred disrupt them. So he cursed them and so it fell out; for
from that day to this the people of Eirinn have never failed to
quarrel in the face of a foe."[26]

O'Duffy also combines Irish mythology and fantasy when he introduces the cryptic *geasa* that the goddess of war Badb lays upon Cuandine as he prepares for battles that will not be limited to hand-to-hand combat, as in tradition. Cuandine later unwittingly breaks three *geasa* when he "kills a lion" (Goshawk) but "spares a jackal" (Slawmy Cander); when he "answers questions of White upon the lips of Black" (answers Cander); and when he contends with the "headless Men of the Wood" (economists). O'Duffy fuses the mythological age with the modern one in a passage reminiscent of the one in which Cuandine tries to explain who he is to the Irish, in *King Goshawk and the Birds*. In *Asses in Clover*, the hero writes to the Minister of Wars, explaining that he has been commissioned by Badb to deliver his people from the enemy. The response, as might be expected, is that the official has no idea who this Badb might be and that any attempt to seek personal influence is unacceptable. The gods and heroes are long forgotten, and their principles have been abandoned.

But Cuandine persists in his mission, and with the heroic air vessel, the Polorketes, whose wings are woven of silk by the women of the *sidhe*, and his sword, the Cruaidin Cailidcheann, Cuandine defeats the International Air Force. Cuandine jumps into battle, using the hero halo, chanting a heroic song, and throwing a distorting fit. He also maintains the convention of threes, with his feats of strength divided into three hard wounds dealt to him and encircling Ireland three times after his victory. The warrior hero also executes the "Scouring of Dublin," a cathartic exercise that O'Duffy calls one of the three great feats of scavenging; he stirs up a powerful wind that cleans the filthy city and defrocks the embarrassed citizens who had failed to support their homeland.

Unlike the conclusion of the first part of the trilogy, in which Cuandine triumphs over evil after humiliating the Wolfian leader, the results of war in the next two novels are progressively disillusioning. In *The Spacious Adventures of the*

Man in the Street, O'Kennedy had failed miserably in a senseless war in space, although admittedly he was not a hero in the manner of Cuchulainn. In *Asses in Clover*, Cuandine, through his dealings with Slawmy Cander, breaks all of his interdictions and nearly fails to free the birds. It is unclear whether O'Duffy intends to point to heroic hubris by introducing these flaws, or whether he builds toward a conclusion that the entire ordeal was not worth the heroic effort. When Cuandine finally tries to liberate the birds, they are so accustomed to their captivity that, like humans who have adjusted to colonial dominance or a stultifying socioeconomic system, they resist change and fight him off.

Cuandine ultimately preoccupies himself with domestic matters, while the well-traveled O'Kennedy, newly inspired with ideas of interplanetary and lunar journeys, partakes in a master plan to colonize and industrialize the moon. The venture is destined to fail, for the moon settlement scheme creates competition and engenders the final war of O'Duffy's trilogy, a war in which total annihilation occurs. The contrived earth-moon battle lacks the poignancy of the breaking of Cuandine's spirit. This event occurs in a very brief chapter that actually articulates how irreconcilable the differences are between Celtic heroic traditions and customs of the modern age. Cuandine, who has retreated to the Golden Valley, discovers that his twin sons and daughters have been totally corrupted by the forces of capitalism, having all secured jobs in private industry, the new Lunar Trading Company. Like Oisin in Figgis' *Return of the Hero*, Cuandine gives up on the civilization he has witnessed (and in part, spawned) and, taking his mortal wife, quits the earth. "What became of the hero thereafter can never be told, for he was never seen again by mortal eye. Whether he found rest in Tir na nOg, or fresh fields for noble deeds in some corporeal world lit by some better sun, or whether he still rides through space in search of his heart's desire, nobody knows."[27]

It is regrettable that O'Duffy does not conclude the third book of his trilogy with this open-ended passage and its yearning for the return of a hero rather than with the destruction of modern civilization, the extermination of man, and the annihilation of the solar system. The apocalyptic quality of his dénouement seems out of proportion in a series of works in which wars are designed to teach humanity lessons and restore order. O'Duffy's complete pessimism robs the satire of its credibility as a critical treatise; and, if the reader searches for hopefulness in the trilogy, he or she may achieve this only by focussing on the spirit of the author's resuscitated heroes from Celtic myth and folklore.

NOTES

1. Lady Wilde, *Ancient Legends, Mystic Charms, and Superstitions of Ireland* (1925; rpt. New York: Lemma Publishing Corp., 1973), p. 191.

2. Robert Hogan, *Eimar O'Duffy* (Lewisburg, Pa.: Bucknell University Press, 1972), p. 55.

3. Eimar O'Duffy, *King Goshawk and the Birds* (London: Macmillan and Co., 1926), p. 6.

4. Ibid., pp. 37-38.

5. Ibid., p. 69.

6. Ibid., p. 77.

7. Vivian Mercier, "The Satires of Eimar O'Duffy," *The Bell* 12, no. 4 (1946), p. 330.

8. *King Goshawk and the Birds*, p. 154.

9. Ibid., p. 171.

10. Ibid., p. 215.

11. Ibid., p. 220.

12. Eimar O'Duffy, *The Spacious Adventures of the Man in the Street* (London: Macmillan and Co., 1928), p. 66.

13. Ibid., p. 215.

14. Ibid., p. 71.

15. Mercier, "The Satires of Eimar O'Duffy," p. 331.

16. *The Spacious Adventures of the Man in the Street*, p. 89.

17. Ibid., p. 311.

18. Wilde, *Ancient Legends*, p. 148.

19. *The Spacious Adventures of the Man in the Street*, pp. 380-381.

20. Ibid., p. 386.

21. Hogan, *Eimar O'Duffy* (Lewisburg: Bucknell University Press, 1972), p. 78.

22. Eimar O'Duffy, *Asses in Clover* (London: Putnam, 1933), p. 38.

23. Ibid., p. 114.

24. Ibid., p. 59.

25. Ibid., p. 160.

26. Ibid., p. 183.

27. Ibid., p. 297.

CHAPTER 7

James Stephens: *The Crock of Gold* and *The Demi-Gods*

James Stephens counted James Joyce among his friends and shared with him an interest in the Gaelic language and a contempt for the organized Church. But his literary approach to the issues of pagan Ireland and Celtic myth, as evidenced in *The Crock of Gold* (1912) and *The Demi-Gods* (1914), does not display the Joycean irreverence for traditions and revivalism. Blending Hellenic, Hibernian, and Hindu motifs, like Joyce, in these early novels, Stephens unites popular folklore with nature and intellect and refrains from blaming an attachment to tradition for Ireland's lack of progress, as well as from reproducing myth tales in literal plot structures, as Yeats did in his less popular dramas. As Patricia McFate observes, James Stephens "brought the gods back to Ireland in *The Crock of Gold*."[1] Reworking folklore in this and the succeeding novel, one in which Yeats saw the hope of Ireland's literary future, Stephens attains synthesis, not because his Irish gods and heroes operate in strict accordance with their original sources but because they serve a purpose that is pragmatic to the plot. Leprechauns, faeries, warrior heroes, and nature gods, immediately recognized as peculiar to Irish legendary source works, are integral to plot development and are not handled by the writer as fading figures from some distant, glorious past.

In his own style of replenishment of Irish literary traditions, James Stephens does not create pure satire or children's literature, although the two novels studied here are sometimes approached in this fashion. Augustine Martin reminds us that Stephens modeled *The Crock of Gold* to some extent after Blake's "Four Zoas," maintaining the many-sided Blakeian personality though several characters, yet omitting an apocalyptic dénouement.[2] He also introduces the theosophical concept that spirits may teach those who are receptive and borrows ideas from Anatole France's *Révolte des Anges*.[3] But Stephens tempers intellectual and didactic features with the amusing interactions of humans with beasts, faery folk, heroes, and gods, so that the reader is ensnared by the fantasy and succumbs to the powers of the Irish world of faery.

In a realistic novel, death by gyration, childswapping, kidnapping, and accusations of murder would belong to the realm of tragedy, but in Stephens' *Crock of Gold*, these plot devices are made comic through the power of the imagination. The reader is continually called upon to overcome astonishment; as Stephens neatly explains in *The Demi-Gods:* "The remarkable thing about astonishment is that it can last for only an instant. No person can be surprised for more than that time."[4] A keen imagination reduces the possibilities of incredulity and hastens our aceptance of the unbelievable.

In *The Crock of Gold*, we learn early on that the wives of the two Philosophers "communicated with each other by a kind of physical telegraphy which they had learned among the Shee— they cracked their finger joints quickly or slowly and so were able to communicate with each other over immense distances."[5] Moreover, the Thin Woman of Inis Magrath can make herself smaller, although she is not quite certain about how to restore herself to original size. Peculiarities, interdictions or *geasa*, and injunctions therefore occur freely in this novel. When Meehawl MacMurrachu complains to the Philosopher that his wife's washboard has been stolen, he reviews a list of ritual actions: he left a pan of milk (for the faeries) on Tuesday; he took off his hat to a dust twirl; his cat had indeed made off with a robin redbreast, hence the broken interdiction. This revelation not only prompts the Philosopher to conclude that the leprechauns of Gort na Cloca Mora have stolen the washboard, for it is strictly forbidden to kill one of their robins, but it synthesizes Irish faery lore with Christian mythology, for the robin is often viewed as a symbol of the bleeding Christ.

Interdiction violation and the commission of sin and their repercussions allow Stephens to develop Irish traditional structural motifs further. Meehawl recovers the missing article, but he also steals the leprechauns' crock of gold, the only treasure they may use for ransom if they are captured by a human. The tiny folk, therefore, must kidnap the Philosopher's children (for it was he who sent Meehawl to the locus of the golden treasure), Seumas and Brigid, since human hands alone may retrieve *The Crock of Gold*. But the children's experience with the leprechauns is such a positive one, for their imaginative abilities grant them innocence, that they promise to visit Gort na Cloca Mora after their release is effected by the Thin Woman. Ironically, the Philosopher has not even perceived his children's absence, for his obsession with intellectual matters has clouded his vision and harmed his imaginative powers, just as his wife's emotionalism has affected her ability to think rationally.

In depicting this struggle between opposing forces and the search for balance, Stephens may be imitating Blake, but he is also espousing a philosophy of the imagination, one he continues to develop in *The Demi-Gods*. Acceptance of the implausible and inexplicable is distinctly Irish, according to Stephens, and best achieved by those who remain simple in spirit: "The McCanns, so far as they professed a religion, were Catholics. Deeper than that, they were Irish folk. From their cradles, if ever they had cradles other than a mother's breast and shoulder, they had supped on wonder. They believed as easily as an animal does, for most creatures are forced to credit everything long before they are able to prove anything."[6] Stephens thus separates religious affiliation from ethnicity, implying a subscription to a faith that is not based on circumspection. Had the Philosopher of *The Crock of Gold* been blessed with the simplemindedness of the McCanns, he too would have partaken of esoteric knowledge without having had to submit to lessons from Pan and Angus Og. But his unshakable faith in intellect must be undermined before he can gain advanced apreciation for nature, his family, and the powers of imagination. Stephens places this faculty under the reign of Angus Og, a Celtic nature god, by which dominion he asserts his superiority to the foreign god of nature, Pan, who answers only to physical desires.

Caitilin, the daughter of Meehawl MacMurrachu, must also suppress her urge to remain satisfied with knowledge and to ignore instinct, when she is forced to choose between Pan and Angus Og for her spouse. Stephens explains:

> She found the Tree of Knowledge, but on every side the great wall soared blackly enclosing her in from the Tree of Life—a wall which her thought was unable to surmount even while instinct urged that it must topple before her advance, but instinct may not advance when thought has schooled it in the science of unbelief; and this wall will not be conqured until until Thought and Instinct are wed, and the first son of that bridal will be called the Scaler of the Wall.[7]

Whether attainable or taboo, intuition, which cannot be found through intellect, becomes a focus again in *The Demi-Gods*. Here Stephens calls it imagination and prophecy, that which humans name "instinct" among the lesser creatures. In *The Crock of Gold*, Caitilin's final decision to remain with Angus Og is a liberating one, for she is not graced with the intuitive abilities of Mary McCann in *The Demi-Gods*. Gary M.

Boyer explains that the world of imagination is "a higher kind of desire, based not simply on appetite but on knowledge and lofty emotion."[8] Indeed, Stephens does not seek to denigrate the fulfillment of such desires of human nature as hunger, love, happiness, and a need for security. But he demonstrates that leprechauns have a greater value than a "Prime Minister or a stockbroker, because a leprechaun dances and makes merry, while a Prime Minister knows nothing of these virtues."[9] Further, he asserts that retribution or satisfaction for personal injury is necessary when *geis* have been broken. When the leprechauns are "forced" to frame the Philosopher for the alleged murder of the other Philosopher and his wife, in order to recover the missing crock of gold and exact revenge, Stephens treats the plan as a necessary evil and dismisses any possible censure. Even though her husband risks hanging for a crime he did not commit, the Thin Woman also absolves the leprechauns of any wrongdoing before she sets off to seek help from Angus Og. In so doing, she separates the Sin from the Sinners, recognizes taboo, and fuses pagan and Christian ideology.

The Thin Woman's bad-tempered disposition can be forgiven in light of her innocent and forthright manners. When her children question her about the ownership of a cow, she replies: "The cow owns herself for nobody can own a thing that is alive. I am sure she gives her milk to us with great good will, for we are modest, temperate people without greed or pretension."[10] Stephens echoes the values of Irish traditional myths and folktales that are asserted by late nineteenth- and early twentieth-century collectors and recorders of source tales. As Augustine Martin notes, these qualities include a plea for poetry and the imagination versus materialism and philistinism.[11]

Stephens' deliberate use of poetic rather than prosaic language is designed to promote openminded innocence and imagination, the absence of which traits led to the first Philosopher's self-imposed death. He lamented: "There is no

longer an horizon before my eyes. Space has narrowed to the
petty dimensions of my thumb. Time is the tick of the
clock."[12] Stephens' vision calls for the ability of humans to
communicate with animals and to observe animals of different
species in conversation with each other and he develops these
ideas in *The Crock of Gold* and *The Demi-Gods*. In the former
work, Seamus and Brigid, who have befriended the leprechauns
and returned their gold to them, endeavor to converse with a
cow and play at being cows themselves. Stephens uses their
naive game to introduce an amusing dialogue that takes place
between a cow and a fly, one that is overheard and understood
by the children and the Thin Woman. Earlier in the same
work, we had to stretch our own imaginations and listen to a
conversation between an ass and a spider. The donkey complains of bachelorhood, while the spider complains of the per-
ils of being wed to a female spider (a possible lighthearted reference to the taboo of the female). While it is certain that Stephens intends for us to find humor in the passage with the spider, he reinforces Gaelic lore through the device. In the spider's
lament we are brought to reflect on the mysterious power of
the female; if the daughters of the goddess Danaan inherit the
powers of life and knowledge, they preserve them and part
with them only under emotional stress. When the Philosopher's wife gives full vent to her anger, she comes into full possession of her knowledge, cursing her spouse with the fourteen
maledictions that are known only to women. When the Thin
Woman takes the children in search of Angus Og, she instructs
Brigid that:

A man must hate all women before he is able to love a woman,
but that he is at liberty, or rather he is under express command, to
love all men because they are of his kind. Women should also love
all other women as themselves, and they should hate all men but one
man only, and him they should seek to turn into a woman, because
women, by the order of their beings, must be either tyrants or
slaves, and it is better they should be tyrants than slaves.[13]

She goes on to speak of the unrelenting warfare between the sexes and of woman's defeat because of her tendency toward pity.

Stephens' women echo Medb's powerful voice in the *Tain*, and Joyce's captivating female, Molly Bloom of *Ulysses*. The Thin Woman of *The Crock of Gold* exercises supernatural powers through her affiliation with the *Shee* and her natural powers of motherhood. She shows no fear of the Three Absolutes, whom, McFate reminds us, parallel Blake's "Ancient Britons,"[14] and she secures the help her husband needs from the Brugh of Angus Mac an Og, son of Dagda Mor. Caitilin ni Murrachu, though a mortal, is desperately needed by Angus Og, who laments that humans have forgotten him. And Stephens' female characters in *The Demi-Gods* also show no fear of otherwordly beings, perhaps drawing their strength from women in Irish source works.

Because temporal realities and factual events pale alongside atemporal realms in Stephens' first two novels, the Philosopher's release from prison, like other plot details, is relatively insignificant. It is the series of mystical and magical events that precede his liberation that points to the importance of Irish pagan values in the deliverance of the country from other entrapments, social, economic, intellectual, or colonial. And the continued precedence of Gaelic heroes as interceders indicates that no foreign mythological figure can effect this liberation.

The Three Absolutes may be Blakeian in inspiration, but they also recall the Christian trinity and the Gaelic triad. The three messages the Philosopher must deliver after his visit with Angus Og go to MacCul, MacCulain, and MacCushin. Because "mac" means "son" in Gaelic, these are easily interpreted as messages to be sent to the sons of Fionn MacCumhaill, Cuchulainn, and Oisin, three great Irish heroes. Fittingly, too, a triumvirate of angels appears to a party of three (if we include the donkey) in the first chapter of *The Demi-Gods* and guide the characters of the novel to self-awareness and happiness in love.

Judgment may be doled out by Rhadamanthus, and evil figures such as Brien O'Brien may carry Hindu karma through their reincarnations, in *The Demi-Gods,* but there is clearly a Gaelic claim on heaven in this novel. Stephens explains: "It was also believed in ancient times, and the belief was world-wide, that the entrance to heaven, hell, and purgatory yawned in the Isle of the Saints, and this belief also, although it has never been proved, has never been disproved, and it does assist the theory that Irish is the celestial language."[15]

Patsy McCann the tinker and his daughter Mary may readily accept that the angel Finaun's creation tale resembles the Gaelic myth of Conan, in which an ongoing sexual metamorphosis occurs through intermittent sex role reversal. Additionally, the struggle between the sexes reechoes the explanation of the Thin Woman in *The Crock of Gold,* the Blakeian quest for balance between opposing forces, and possibly Joyce's experimentation with Bloom's switching gender in *Ulysses.* But Stephens' somewhat hazy story of creation resembles the Christian myth of Adam, too, in that the acquisition of knowledge heralds the condition of sin: "for in that space knowledge had put forth a bud and a blossom and she looked through knowledge. She saw herself and the demon and the man, and she prayed to the demon."[16] While knowledge is attained by both man and woman, in a Faustian manner, special sight is still reserved for the woman. Stephens demonstrates that Patsy's thirst for leadership allows him to wield what is but token power, for his daughter possesses magical gifts and exercises true control. When the angels first appear, we are told: "She did not appear to be taking any heed of the strangers, but it is likely that she was able to see them without looking, because, as is well known, women and birds are able to see without turning their heads, and that is indeed a necessary provision, for they are both surrounded by enemies."[17] The young girl, who so gently communicates with the beast of burden, appoints herself "mother" of four men: her father and the angels,

Finaun, Caeltia, and Art. Mary McCann may be a recreation of Caitilin ni Murrachu, grown stronger or more aware of her strength. She craves the power of the Gaelic goddess but, Stephens explains, can never use it once it has been attained. Like the weakening effect pity has in *The Crock of Gold*, gentleness diminishes woman's strength in *The Demi-Gods*, yet the power is ever yielded to the female. This magnetic force may draw Art, the youngest angel, back to Mary when the others return to heaven at the novel's end. Whatever intuitive power she commands, it certainly enables her to dominate her father, who, in spite of teasing and recriminations, follows her every order.

There is yet another power vested in woman that makes a slave of Patsy McCann—the sensual hold that creates lust. In one of the tinker's more whimsical and honest exchanges with his guardian angel, Caeltia, McCann admits that he is jealous of Eileen ni Cooley:

> "She's a bad woman," replied Patsy.
> "What sort of bad woman is she?"
> "She's the sort that commits adultery with every kind of man," said he harshly. Caeltia turned over that accusation for a moment.
> "Did she ever commit adultery with yourself?" said he.
> "She did not," said Patsy, "and that's why I don't like her."
> "I think," said he, "that the reason you don't like that woman is because you like her too much."[18]

The feisty woman, through the guidance of her own guardian angel, Finaun, eventually returns to Patsy McCann, whom she recognizes as a decent man, once he is rid of human greed, a vice that haunts provincial types as well as sophisticates.

There is a fair amount of preoccupation with property in *The Demi-Gods*, just as there are arguments of ownership in *The Crock of Gold*. But while the leprechauns' treasure had been amassed to safeguard their freedom, fortunes acquired by ordinary humans merely satisfy a thirst for ownership and/or

power. Billy the Music attests to the principle often stated in
Irish folklore: just enough money guarantees security, but excess wealth creates a burden (even though this may be an attempt at consolation for the poor). Patsy McCann, as a wanderer, is nearly free of the enslavement created by property,
yet he is tempted from time to time by the brilliance of gold.
Stephens describes the oppressiveness of acquisitions with respect to the angels and McCann: "They had not property and
so they had no prejudices, for the person who has nothing may
look upon the world as his inheritance, while the person who
has something has seldom anything but that."[19]

Billy the Music speaks of sacrosanct faery gold and is liberated from selfish pettiness when he renounces his wealth and
takes to the road with his concertina. Brien O'Brien, on the
other hand, unable to rid himself of attachment to pecuniary
matters, is juxtaposed against McCann. Patsy is aware of the
proper disposition of money and commits the three-penny
piece to the body of deceased O'Brien, whom he duly inters.
As Martin notes, the judgment of the avaricious O'Brien is
more complicated than that of Yeats' "Fiddler of Dooney."[20]
Stephens replaces St. Peter with Rhadamanthus and tosses
O'Brien out of heaven in the company of Cuchulain the Seraph, who claims to be the guardian angel of Billy the Music.
The author inventively uses the Gaelic warrior hero to chastise
Billy for his greed, consort with the thievish O'Brien on earth,
and display heroic peculiarities. When Rhadamanthus commands Cuchulain to surrender gold, the Irish hero begins a fit
of distortion: "Let them come and take it from me, said the
seraph Cuchulain. And suddenly (for these things are at the
will of the spirits) around his head the lightning spun, and his
hands were on the necks of thunders."[21] Although quelled by
the god of judgment, Cuchulain grows strong because he defies
control of a foreign god. He has been reduced in power but
not in spirit.

Often, by contrast, Stephens attributes powers of the faery

world to the humblest creatures, such as the donkey, who lis-
tens to all conversations, "no matter who was being talked to,
and not a person objected to him."[22] This contemplative but
unassuming creature delivers the blow that puts Brien O'Brien
to rest again, accomplishing with his two heels what the fists of
Eileen and Patsy cannot. Similarly, the dogs of young Tomas
in *The Crock of Gold* had attacked the policeman who was
about to wrongfully incarcerate the Philosopher, earning his
esteem for their wisdom and intuition. The youngest demi-
god, Art, also displays respect for members of the animal kingdom when he enters into earnest conversation with a spider
and wishes him luck in his endeavors. Art has been blessed
with the open imagination of Mary McCann, although he is,
curiously, the weakest of the storytellers in *The Demi-Gods*.
Art's lack of experience in the oral tradition of the Gaelic *seanachie* is contrasted to the gift of the native storyteller, whose
secret is revealed to Billy the Music: "He would tell you a
thing you knew all your life, and you would think it was a
new thing. There was no age in that man's mind, and that's the
secret of storytelling."[23] And, as Patricia McFate accurately observes, Finaun, Billy the Music, Caeltia, and Art all try their
hand at tale-weaving, drawing from sources other than Gaelic
ones. But each time, the audience responds as to a traditional
seanachie.[24] There is a patient willingness to hear the familiar
plot retold by different tellers; listening to the recitation of the
fate of Brien O'Brien and Cuchulain the Seraph is made more
interesting because of each teller's narrative technique.

The realization that plots, structures, and themes are continually reworked allows us to observe the circular and repeti-
tive nature of *The Demi-Gods*, which, like *The Return of the
Hero* and *Finnegans Wake*, ends where it has begun (in this instance, with the angels retrieving their belongings). Geographi-
cally, McCann and his daughter have traced a circle in the Irish
countryside; spiritually, their lives have been enriched by the
intervention of *The Crock of Gold* (from whom Patsy nearly

stole all their material goods); and they have been entertained with various renditions of a basic tale of good and evil. Stephens has resultantly become a modern-age *seanachie*, one who perceives that the reader does not necessarily object to some degree of narrative predictability, for who can resist a new spin on an old plot, and he achieves what Yeats esteemed in his writing: "the use of Irish mythology and folklore in a new imaginative context."[25]

NOTES

1. Patricia McFate, *The Writings of James Stephens* (New York: St. Martin's, 1979), p. 11.

2. Augustine Martin, *James Stephens: A Critical Study* (Totowa, N. J.: Rowman and Littlefield, 1977), p. 38.

3. McFate, *The Writings of James Stephens*, p. 52.

4. James Stephens, *The Demi-Gods* (London: Macmillan and Co.. 1914), p. 15.

5. James Stephens, *The Crock of Gold* (1912; rpt. New York: Macmillan Co., 1936), p. 6.

6. *The Demi-Gods*, p. 16.

7. *The Crock of Gold*, p. 138.

8. Gary M. Boyer, "*The Crock of Gold*," *Antigonish Review* 4 (1980), p. 94.

9. *The Crock of Gold*, p. 156.

10. Ibid., p. 269.

11. Martin, *James Stephens: A Critical Study*, p. 48.

12. *The Crock of Gold*, p. 15.

13. Ibid., pp. 262-263.

14. McFate, *The Writings of James Stephens*, p. 41.

15. *The Demi-Gods*, p. 69.

16. Ibid., p. 106.

17. Ibid., p. 14.

18. Ibid., p. 79.

19. Ibid., p. 53.

20. Martin, *James Stephens: A Critical Study*, p. 77.

21. *The Demi-Gods*, p. 178.

22. Ibid., p. 263.

23. Ibid., p. 185.

24. McFate, *The Writings of James Stephens*, p. 146.

25. Richard J. Finneran, *The Olympian and the Leprechaun: W. B. Yeats and James Stephens* (Dublin: Dolmen Press, 1978), p. 22.

Conclusion

Richard J. Finneran creates a well-constructed argument to explain how and why nationality intrudes in the literature of Ireland. According to his theory, the first approach a writer takes is didactic, in the interest of propaganda; the second approach is mimetic, a superficial nationalism at best; and the third approach is symbiotic, when nationality and literature become interdependent and exist in reciprocal relationship.[1] He then goes on to explain that the work of James Stephens progressed from that of a didactic nature to a symbiotic one after 1914, at which point in his career Stephens began to make direct use of tales from the Fenian Cycle and the *Tain* epic.[2] But Finneran fails to entertain the use of motifs from Gaelic folklore, the devices of interdiction, metamorphosis, peculiarity, and superstition, and their fusion with devices from Catholic doctrine in his consideration of *The Crock of Gold* and *The Demi-Gods*, which allow the novels to transcend the mimetic mode and achieve symbiosis. If one purpose of folklore, particularly the folklore of a people who have undergone colonization, is to validate their culture, then the integration of motifs from that folklore in literature marks the writing as peculiarly from that culture.

   The interdependence of literature and nationality occurs in all twelve novels considered in this study. While they all preserve patterns of Irish folklore, their purposes and techniques vary, ranging from parody, pastiche, satire, and fantasy to mimesis and didactic plot repetition. Joyce imitates narrative techniques of oral tradition, reinvents the quarrel of Oisin and St. Patrick, to some degree, in both *Ulysses* and *Finnegans Wake*, and experiments with familiar tales from a culture he knew best. Darrell Figgis also recreates the Ossianic debate, but in a more straightforward manner and with more biting satire. Joyce's introduction of language play, with his puns, sigla, metatheses, and riddles, veils the satire and obscures the source works; Figgis' point-by-point plot structure denies the possibility of other sources.

   Mervyn Wall and Eimar O'Duffy both dabble in satire, but also go into the realm of fantasy in their Irish novels. Wall claims to have had a fondness for Greek mythology as a youth and to have been exposed to Fenian lore primarily through the Revivalist writings of Yeats, Lady Gregory, and Æ.[3] Yet the wanderings of his hero Fursey are Ossianic in that the outcast attains an imbalance through his belief in Christian values and association with pagan forces. O'Duffy makes a stronger case for a return to traditional values of the Celtic warrior hero, such as Cuchulainn, but his overall pessimism prevents his trilogy from achieving the fanciful qualities of the Fursey novels. O'Duffy's hero is given express injunctions and, in the mythic mode, suffers greatly when they are not completed; Wall's hero stumbles into situations of peculiarity and interdiction but manages to scrape by without mortal injury. Yet both writers exploit motifs from the newly revived mythology of a self-absorbed culture bent on catching up on its own history and asserting its heritage.

   Flann O'Brien may be the most whimsical of the authors vis-à-vis his approach to Irish myth and legend. His Finn MacCool has somehow gotten mixed in with a cast of extras from a

Western movie set, unlikely companions for a warrior hero; and his Sweeny, in *At Swim-Two-Birds*, interrupts the plot, reproducing bardic chant from his perch in a tree.

Devices such as those discussed in this study are, arguably, evident in the bodies of folk and faery tales the world over. But it is difficult to find a body of literature outside Ireland that avails itself so readily of its folklore, relying upon stereotypical motifs for artistic and commercial purposes. Even the literature of writers who lived abroad and spent some time in areas where Gaelic narratives were recited reflects the influence of that acculturization, as evidenced in Sidney's *Arcadia* and Sterne's *Tristram Shandy*. The connection between Laurence Sterne and James Joyce has long been recognized, for Dorothy VanGhent suggests that *Finnegans Wake* realizes the potentialities of linguistic play and the dream motif of Sterne's novel,[4] and we may connect the fantasy to an Irish upbringing. Strategies of the Gaelic storyteller are best repeated by those writers who listened to the source tale, as Joyce had with his own father.

But even those writers who admit minimal exposure to Irish folklore, via written sources, are capable of being influenced by the Mythological, Ulster, and Fenian Cycle tales. Scholarly translations of Gaelic works of antiquity, in the tradition of Kuno Meyer and Heinrich Zimmer, became popularized in the manner of Standish O'Grady, who, Richard Fallis explains, used the raw materials of the scholars imaginatively to recreate Irish life and legend.[5] Scholarly recordings, popular renditions, and literary innovations of Irish myth and folklore all assert the persistence of the source works in the written mode. And the modern writer, who owes a debt to translators, chroniclers, and popularizers, maintains the structures and themes of these stories in his own literature. In doing so, he guarantees the continuance of this cultural wellspring.

NOTES

1. Richard J. Finneran, "Literature and Nationality in the Work of James Stephens," *South Atlantic Bulletin* 4, no. 4 (1975), pp. 18-19.

2. Ibid., p. 23.

3. Mervyn Wall, unpublished notes.

4. Dorothy VanGhent, *The English Novel* (1953; rpt. New York: Harper and Row, 1961), p. 86.

5. Richard Fallis, *The Irish Renaissance* (Syracuse: Syracuse University Press, 1977), p. 62.

Selected Bibliography

Alter, Robert. *Partial Magic: The Novel as a Self-Conscious Genre*. Berkeley: University of California Press, 1976.

apRoberts, Ruth. *"At Swim-Two-Birds* and the Novel as Self-Evident Sham." *Éire/Ireland* 6, no. 2 (1971), 76-97.

Beechhold, Henry F. "Joyce's Otherworld." *Éire/Ireland* 1 (1972), 103-115.

Begnal, Michael. "The Fables of *Finnegans Wake*." *James Joyce Quarterly* 6 (1969), 357-367.

———. "The Narrator of *Finnegans Wake*." *Éire/Ireland* 4, no. 3 (1969), 38-49.

Begnal, Michael, and Eckley, Grace. *Narrator and Character in Finnegans Wake*. Lewisburg, Pa.: Bucknell University Press, 1975.

Benstock, Bernard. "The Three Faces of Brian O'Nolan," in *Alive-Alive-O!: Flann O'Brien's "At Swim-Two-Birds,"* ed. Rüdiger Imhof. Totowa, N. J.: Barnes and Noble, 1985, 59-70.

Bowen, Zack. *Ulysses as a Comic Novel*. Syracuse: Syracuse University Press, 1989.

Bowen, Zack, and Carens, James, eds. *A Companion to Joyce Studies*. Westport, Conn.: Greenwood Press, 1984.

Boyer, Gary M. *"The Crock of Gold." Antigonish Review* 4 (1980), 91-99.

Burgess, Anthony. *Joysprick*. London: Andre Deutsch, 1973. New York: W. W. Norton and Co., 1965.

———. *ReJoyce*. New York: W. W. Norton and Co., 1965.

Bushrui, Suheil Badi, and Benstock, Bernard, eds. *James Joyce: An*

International Perspective. Totowa, N. J.: Barnes and Noble, 1982.

Campbell, Joseph, and Robinson, Henry M. *A Skeleton Key to Finnegans Wake*. New York: Harcourt, Brace, 1944.

Clissman, Anne. *Flann O'Brien: A Critical Introduction to His Writings*. New York: Barnes and Noble, 1975.

Cross, Tom Peete, and Slover, Clark Harris, eds. *Ancient Irish Tales*. New York: Barnes and Noble, 1936.

Cumpiano, Marion. "Dolphins and Dolphin's Barn: The Womb of Youth in *Ulysses* and *Finnegans Wake*." *Dutch Quarterly Review of Anglo-American Letters* 11, no. 2 (1981), 134-144.

De Jubainville, H. d'Arbois. *The Irish Mythological Cycle and Celtic Mythology,* trans. Richard Irvine Best. Dublin: O'Donoghue and Co., 1903.

Delaney, Frank. *The Celts*. Boston: Little, Brown, and Co., 1986.

Dundes, Alan. *The Study of Folklore*. Englewood Cliffs, N. J.: Prentice-Hall, 1965.

Dunn, John J. "Darrell Figgis, a Man Nearly Anonymous." *Journal of Irish Literature* 1 (1986), 33-42.

Eckley, Grace. "'Between Peas Like Ourselves': The Folklore of the Prankquean." *James Joyce Quarterly* 9 (1972), 177-188.

Ellmann, Richard. *James Joyce*. New York: Oxford University Press, 1982.

Fackler, Herbert V. *That Tragic Queen: The Deirdre Legend in Anglo-Irish Literature*. Salzburg: Institut für Englische Sprache und Literatur, 1978.

Fallis, Richard. *The Irish Renaissance*. Syracuse: Syracuse University Press, 1977.

Finneran, Richard J. "Literature and Nationality in the Work of James Stephens." *South Atlantic Bulletin* 4, no. 4 (1975), 18-25.

———. *The Olympian and the Leprechaun: W. B. Yeats and James Stephens*. Dublin: Dolmen Press, 1978.

Flower, Robin. *The Irish Tradition*, 2nd ed., 1947; rpt. Oxford: Clarendon Press, 1948.

Garvin, John. "Some Irish and Anglo-Irish Allusions in *Finnegans Wake*." *James Joyce Quarterly* 11 (1974), 266-278.

Gifford, Don, and Seidman, Robert J. *Notes for Joyce*. New York: E. P. Dutton and Co., 1974.

Glasheen, Adaline. *Third Census of Finnegans Wake*. Berkeley: University of California Press, 1977.

Gose, Elliott B., Jr. *The World of the Irish Wonder Tale*. Toronto: University of Toronto Press, 1985.

Hart, Clive. *Structure and Motif in Finnegans Wake*. Evanston, Ill: Northwestern University Press, 1962.

Henderson, Gordon. "An Interview with Mervyn Wall." *Journal of Irish Literature* 11, no. 1 (1982), 3-18.

Hogan, Robert. *Eimar O'Duffy*. Lewisburg, Pa.: Bucknell University Press, 1972.

———. *Mervyn Wall*. Lewisburg Pa.: Bucknell University Press, 1972.

———. "Mervyn Wall." In *Supernatural Fiction Writers: Fantasy and Horror*, vol. 2, ed. E. F. Bleiler. New York: Charles Scribner's Sons, 1985, 645-650.

Imhof, Rüdiger. *Alive-Alive O!: Flann O'Brien's At Swim-Two-Birds*. Totowa, N. J.: Barnes and Noble, 1985.

Ireland, Michael. *The Return of the Hero*. London: Chapman and Dodd, 1923.

Jeffares, Norman. *Anglo-Irish Literature*. New York: Schocken, 1982.

Jones, Stephen, ed. *A Flann O'Brien Reader*. New York: Viking, 1978.

Joyce, James. *Finnegans Wake*. 1939; rpt. New York: Viking, 1967.

———. *Ulysses*. Edited by Hans Walter Gabler. New York: Garland, 1981.

Kelleher, John V. "Identifying the Irish Printed Sources for *Finnegans Wake*." *Irish University Review* 1, no. 2 (1971), 161-177.

Kenner, Hugh. *Joyce's Voices*. Berkeley: University of California Press, 1978.

Kiberd, Declan. "The Vulgarity of Heroics," in *James Joyce: An International Perspective*, ed. Suheil Bushrui and Bernard Benstock. Totowa: N. J.: Barnes and Noble, 1982, 156-159.

Kilroy, Thomas. "Mervyn Wall: The Demands of Satire." *Studies* 47 (1958), 83-89.

Kinsella, Thomas, trans. *Tain bo Cuailgne*. Oxford: Oxford University Press, 1970.

Krause, David. *The Profane Book of Irish Comedy*. Ithaca, N. Y.: Cornell University Press, 1982.

Lawrence, Karen. *The Odyssey of Style in Ulysses*. Princeton: Princeton University Press, 1981.

Lee, L. L. "The Dublin Cowboys of Flann O'Brien." *Western American Literature* 4 (1969), 219-225.

Lévi-Strauss, Claude. *Myth and Meaning*. New York: Schocken, 1979.

Levin, Harry. *James Joyce: A Critical Introduction*. Norfolk, Va.: New Directions, 1941.

MacKillop, James. *Fionn MacCumhaill: Celtic Myth in English Literature*. Syracuse: Syracuse University Press, 1986.

MacLochlainn, Alf. "Eimar O'Duffy: A Bibliographical Biography." *The Irish Book* 1, no. 1 (1958), 37-47.

MacNamara, Desmond. *The Book of Intrusions*. Normal, Ill.: Dalkey Press, 1994.

Marcus, Phillip L. "Conchubar MacNessa and *Finnegans Wake*." *Wake Newslitter* 4 (1967), 36-37.

———. "Notes on Irish Elements in 'Scylla and Charybdis.'" *James Joyce Quarterly* 10 (1973), 312-320.

———. "Three Irish Allusions in *Ulysses*." *James Joyce Quarterly* 6 (1969), 299-305.

Martin, Augustine. *James Stephens: A Critical Study*. Totowa, N.J.: Rowman and Littlefield, 1977.

McCarthy, Patrick. "The Structures and Meanings of *Finnegans Wake*," in *A Companion to Joyce Studies*, ed. Zack Bowen and James Carens. Westport, Conn.: Greenwood Press, 1984, 559-632.

McFate, Patricia. *The Writings of James Stephens*. New York: St. Martin's, 1979.

McGuire, Jerry L. "Teasing after Death: Metatextuality in *The Third Policeman*." *Éire/Ireland* 16, no. 2 (1981), 107-121.

Mercier, Vivian. *The Irish Comic Tradition*. Oxford: Oxford University Press, 1962.

———. "The Satires of Eimar O'Duffy." *The Bell* 12, no. 4 (1946), 325-336.

Meyer, Kuno, ed. and trans. *The Vision of MacConglinne: A Middle Irish Wonder Tale*. David Nutt, 1892; rpt. New York: Lemma Publishing Corp., 1974.

Mietzner, Hartmut. *Immanenz und Transzendenz in Joyces Portrait of the Artist and Ulysses*. Frankfurt am Main: Peter Lang, 1978.

Morse, J. Mitchell. *The Sympathetic Alien: James Joyce and Catholicism*. New York: New York University Press, 1959.

Murphy, Gerard. *The Ossianic Lore and Romantic Tales of Medieval Ireland*. Dublin: Colm O'Lochlainn, 1961.

Nagy, Joseph Falaky. *The Wisdom of the Outlaw*. Berkeley: University of California Press, 1985.

Norris, Margot. *The Decentered Universe of Finnegans Wake*. Baltimore: Johns Hopkins University Press, 1974.

———. "The Function of Mythic Repetition in *Finnegans Wake*." *James Joyce Quarterly* 11 (1974), 343-354.

O'Brien, Edna. "Why Irish Heroines Don't Have to be Good Anymore." *New York Times Book Review* 11 (May 1986), 13.

O'Brien, Flann. *At Swim-Two-Birds*. New York: Pantheon, 1939.

———. *The Dalkey Archive*. New York: Macmillan Co., 1964.

———. *The Third Policeman*. 1940; rpt. New York: Walker and Co., 1967.

O'Connor, Frank. *A Short History of Irish Literature*. New York: G. P. Putnam's Sons, 1967.

O'Duffy, Eimar. *Asses in Clover*. London: Putnam, 1933.

———. *King Goshawk and the Birds*. London: Macmillan and Co., 1926.

———. *The Spacious Adventures of the Man in the Street*. London: Macmillan and Co., 1928.

O'Grady, Thomas B. "*At Swim-Two-Birds* and the Bardic Schools." *Éire/Ireland* 24, no. 3 (1989), 65-77.

O'Hara, Patricia. "Finn MacCool and the Bard's Lament in Flann O'Brien's *At Swim-Two-Birds*." *Journal of Irish Literature* 15, no. 1 (1986), 55-61.

O'Hehir, Brendan. "ALP's Gaelic Ancestry." *James Joyce Quarterly* 2 (1965), 158-166.

———. *A Gaelic Lexicon for Finnegans Wake and a Glossary for Joyce's Other Works*. Berkeley: University of California Press, 1967.

———. "O Connochar, O Conchobhair, Conchobhar." *Wake Newslitter* 4 (1967), 67-71.

O'Rahilly, Thomas F. *Early Irish History and Mythology*. 1946; rpt. Dublin: Dublin Institute for Advanced Studies, 1971.

O'Sullivan, Sean. *The Folklore of Ireland*. New York: Hastings House, 1974.

Paterakis, Deborah T. "Mananaan MacLir in *Ulysses*." *Éire/Ireland* 7, no. 3 (1972), 29-35.

Peterson, Richard F. "Flann O'Brien's Timefoolery." *Irish Renaissance Annual* 3 (1982), 30-46.

Power, Patrick C. *A Literary History of Ireland*. Cork: Mercier Press, 1969.

Propp, Vladimir. *Morphology of the Folktale*, 2nd ed., 1958; rpt. Austin: University of Texas Press, 1968.

Quintelli-Neary, Marguerite. "Desmond MacNamara's Intrusions and Invasions." *Notes on Modern Irish Literature* 8 (1996), 25-30.

Riquelme, John. *Teller and Tale in Joyce's Fiction*. Baltimore: Johns Hopkins University Press, 1983.

Sawyer, Ruth. *The Way of the Storyteller*. Middlesex, Eng.: Penguin, 1942.

Scott, Bonnie Kime. *James Joyce*. Atlantic Highlands, N.J.: Humanities Press International, 1987.

Senn, Fritz. "Old Celtic Romances." *Wake Newslitter* 4 (1957), 8-10.

Silverthorne, J. M. "Time, Literature, and Failure: Flann O'Brien's *At Swim-Two-Birds* and *The Third Policeman*." *Éire/Ireland* 2, no. 4 (1976), 66-83.

Sjoestedt-Jonval, Marie-Louise. *Dieux et héros des celtes*. Paris: Presses universitaires de France, 1940.

Stephens, James. *The Crock of Gold*. 1912; rpt. New York: Macmillan Co., 1936.

———. *The Demi-Gods*. London: Macmillan and Co., 1914.

Stokes, Whitley, trans. *The Tripartite Life of St. Patrick with Other Documents Relating to the Saint*. London: Eyre and Spottiswoode, 1887.

Sullivan, Charles W., III. *Welsh Celtic Myth in Modern Fantasy*. Westport, Conn.: Greenwood Press, 1989.

Sultan, Stanley. "An Old Irish Model for *Ulysses*." *James Joyce Quarterly* 5 (1968), 103-109.

Taylor, Archer. "The Biographical Pattern in Traditional Narrative." *Journal of the Folklore Institute* 1, no. 1 (1964), 114-129.

Thornton, Weldon. *Allusions in Ulysses*. Chapel Hill: University of North Carolina Press, 1962.

Thuente, Mary Helen. "'Traditional Innovations': Yeats and Joyce and the Irish Oral Tradition." *Mosaic* 12, no. 3 (1979), 91-104.

———. *W.B. Yeats and Folklore*. Totowa, N. J.: Barnes and Noble, 1980.

Tracy, Robert. "Leopold Bloom Fourfold: A Hungarian-Hebraic-Hellenic-Hibernian Hero." *Massachusetts Review* 6 (1965), 523-538.

Tymoczko, Maria. *The Irish Ulysses*. Berkeley: University of California Press, 1994.

VanGhent, Dorothy. *The English Novel*. 1953; rpt. New York: Harper and Row, 1961.

Vickery, John B. *"Finnegans Wake* and Sexual Metamorphosis." *Contemporary Literature* 13 (1972), 213-242.

Voelker, Joseph C. "'Doublends Jined': The Fiction of Flann O'Brien." *Journal of Irish Literature* 12, no. 1 (1983), 87-95.

Wall, Mervyn. *The Return of Fursey.* London: Pilot Press, 1948.

———. *The Unfortunate Fursey.* London: Pilot Press, 1946.

———. Unpublished Notes.

Wilde, Lady Augusta. *Ancient Legends, Mystic Charms and Superstitions of Ireland.* 1925; rpt. New York: Lemma Publishing Corp., 1973.

Index

Diarmaid and Grainne: *Finnegans Wake* and, 67; legend of 6; *The Unfortunate Fursey* and, 105

dinnsenchas, 46, 69

Dubliners, 40

fantasy, 4, 152; Flann O'Brien and, 84; satirical, 99

fennid, 15, 63, 72, 109, 112

fian, 8, 63, 109

Figgis, Darrell, 108, 113

fili, 5, 15, 45, 52, 92, 129

Finnegans Wake, 59–79; *Acallamh na Senorach* and, 62–70, 72–73; *geis* violation in, 70–73, 78

folklore: defined, 1–2, 4; motifs in, 43; purposes of, 3

fomoire, 88, 116

France, Anatole, 138

Gabhra, Battle of, 109

geasa. See geis

geis: *The Crock of Gold* and, 141; defined, 9; *Finnegans Wake* and 60, 62, 70–73, 78; *King Goshawk and the Birds* and, 124, 128; Flann O'Brien and, 89, 91, 93; *The Return of the Hero* and, 110; sexual, 12; *The Spacious Adventures of the Man in the Street* and, 118, 121; *Ulysses* and, 29, 37; *The Unfortunate Fursey* and, 101

Goethe, Johann Wolfgang von. *See* "Walpurgisnacht"

Hamlet: incest in, 44; as pagan source work, 34, 40–41; *Ulysses* and, 30, 48, 71–72

Hyde, Douglas, 42, 45

imbas forosna, 9, 39, 71, 101

imram, 27, 87

Imtheacht na Tromdhaimhe, 30

indarba, 34

Ireland, Michael. *See* Figgis, Darrell

Irish Mythological Cycle, 26, 43

Joyce, James: Cult of Cuchulainn and, 28; H. d'Arbois de Jubainville and, 26; Irishry of, 26; parody and, 30

Joyce, Patrick Weston, 27–28

King Goshawk and the Birds, 7, 115–17

Land of the Young. *See* Tir na nOg

lochlannaig, 88

loidhe, 5

MacCumhaill, Fionn: Fenian legend and, 2; *imbas forosnai* and, 17

macgnimartha, 8, 64, 119

MacLir, Mananaan, 3, 6, 43, 49–51

Medb: Molly Bloom and, 31–32, 54; *Tain bo Cuailgne* and, 10, 31–32;

metamorphosis: *At Swim-Two-Birds* and, 94; *The Crock of*